Game Development with Rust

Advanced Techniques for Building Robust and Efficient, Fast and Fun, Functional Games

Phillips Jeremy

Table of Contents

Preface

Hello, fellow creators! I'm absolutely thrilled you're holding this book in your hands. If you're like me, you're fascinated by the magic of making games, and you're always looking for ways to build them better, faster, and with more confidence. That's exactly what this book is all about. We're going to explore how Rust, with its incredible power and safety, can transform the way we approach game development.

Background and Motivation

Let's be honest, game development can be a wild ride. We want games that run smoothly, look amazing, and don't crash at the most inconvenient times. Traditionally, we've leaned on languages like C++ for performance, but that often comes with a steep price in terms of memory safety and potential bugs. I've personally spent countless hours debugging issues that could've been avoided. That's why I became so excited about Rust. It offers that same raw speed, but with a built-in safety net that lets us focus on what really matters: building fantastic games. I wanted to share my findings, and create a resource that helps others harness the power of Rust.

Purpose and Scope

This book isn't just about learning Rust syntax; it's about applying that knowledge to build real, robust, and performant games. We'll look at advanced techniques, architectural patterns, and optimization strategies that will help you create games that not only run well but are also a joy to develop. We'll cover topics like advanced rendering, physics, audio, and more, all with a focus on practical application.

Target Audience

This book is for those who already have a solid foundation in Rust and some experience with game development concepts. If you've tinkered with game engines before and you're comfortable with Rust's core principles, you're in the right place. We're going to skip the basics and jump right into the good stuff: the advanced techniques that will take your game development skills to the next level. If you're ready to push the limits of what you can create, you'll find plenty to excite you here.

Organization and Structure

We've organized this book into three main parts. First, we'll solidify your understanding of advanced Rust concepts and explore architectural patterns that are essential for building robust games. Then, we'll get our hands dirty building core game systems, focusing on speed and functionality. Finally, we'll add the polish that makes a game truly shine, covering UI, animation, and more. Each chapter is packed with practical examples and code snippets to help you understand and apply the concepts.

Invitation to Read

I'm genuinely excited for you to start this journey with me. My hope is that this book will empower you to create games that are not only technically impressive but also genuinely fun and engaging. Let's get started, and together, we can build some truly amazing things!

Chapter 1: Rust Refresher and Advanced Concepts

Alright, let's kick things off with a solid foundation. We're assuming you've got some Rust under your belt, but even experienced folks can benefit from a quick tune-up and a look at some of the more advanced techniques we'll be using. This chapter is all about getting us on the same page and making sure we're ready to tackle the game development challenges ahead.

1.1 Core Rust Principles Recap

Let's really get into the heart of what makes Rust, well, Rust. We're not just skimming over the basics here; we're going to explore them in detail, so we have a solid foundation for tackling the complexities of game development. Think of this as a relaxed conversation, where we're digging into the nuances of each concept.

Variables and Mutability: The Art of Controlled Change

When you begin writing Rust, you'll immediately notice the let keyword. It's how we introduce variables, but there's more to it than just that. By default, variables in Rust are immutable. This means once a value is assigned, you can't alter it. This might seem like a restriction, but it's a powerful tool for preventing errors.

Consider this scenario: you're developing a game, and a player's score is calculated. You wouldn't want that score to change unexpectedly due to some unintended modification in another part of your code. Immutable variables ensure that this doesn't happen.

However, sometimes you *do* need variables to change. That's where let mut comes in. It explicitly tells the compiler that a variable is mutable, meaning its value can be modified.

```rust
Rust

fn main() {

    let experience_points = 500; // Immutable.
Can't be changed after assignment.

    // experience_points = 550; // This would
cause a compile-time error.



    let mut player_level = 1; // Mutable. Can be
changed.

    player_level = 2; // Perfectly valid.

    println!("Player level: {}", player_level);

}
```

In a game context, experience_points might represent a fixed reward for completing a level, while player_level could change as the player progresses. This control over mutability helps us write more predictable and reliable code.

Data Types: Defining the Shape of Information

Rust is a strongly typed language, which means the compiler needs to know the type of every variable at compile time. This might seem tedious, but it catches errors early, preventing runtime crashes and making debugging easier.

We have a rich set of data types:

- Integers: i8, i16, i32, i64, u8, u16, u32, u64, isize, usize. These represent whole numbers, with signed (i) and unsigned (u) variants. The size variants (8, 16, 32, 64) indicate the number of bits used to store the value. isize and usize depend on the architecture of the computer.

- Floating-Point Numbers: f32, f64. These represent numbers with decimal points. f32 is a 32-bit float, and f64 is a 64-bit float.
- Booleans: bool. These represent true or false values.
- Characters: char. These represent single Unicode characters.
- Strings: String and &str. String is a growable, heap-allocated string, while &str is a string slice, a reference to a sequence of UTF-8 encoded bytes.

Let's illustrate with an example:

Rust

```
fn main() {

    let enemy_id: u32 = 9876;

    let enemy_name: String =
String::from("Goblin");

    let enemy_health: f32 = 75.2;

    let is_boss: bool = false;



    println!("Enemy ID: {}", enemy_id);

    println!("Enemy Name: {}", enemy_name);

    println!("Enemy Health: {}", enemy_health);

    println!("Is Boss: {}", is_boss);

}
```

In a game, enemy_id might be an unsigned integer, enemy_name a string, enemy_health a floating-point number, and is_boss a boolean. Using the right data types ensures that our data is stored and manipulated correctly.

Control Flow: Guiding the Execution Path

Control flow statements allow us to dictate the order in which our code executes. We use if, else, match, for, and while to make decisions and repeat code.

- if and else: These allow us to execute different blocks of code based on conditions.
- match: This allows us to match a value against a pattern and execute corresponding code, especially useful for enums.
- for and while: These allow us to repeat blocks of code.

Here's a practical example:

```Rust
fn main() {

    let player_ammo = 0;


    if player_ammo > 0 {

        println!("Player can shoot!");

    } else {

        println!("Player is out of ammo!");

    }
```

```
for enemy_index in 0..3 {

    println!("Enemy {} spawned!",
enemy_index);

    }

}
```

In a game, if and else might be used to check if the player has ammo, and for loops might be used to spawn multiple enemies.

Structs and Enums: Organizing Data and Choices

Structs and enums are powerful tools for organizing data and representing choices.

- Structs: These allow us to group related data together into custom types.
- Enums: These allow us to represent a value that can be one of several possible variants.

Rust

```
struct Item {

    name: String,

    weight: f32,

    value: u32,

}


enum PlayerAction {

    Attack,
```

```rust
    Defend,

    UseItem(String),

}


fn main() {
    let sword = Item {

        name: String::from("Steel Sword"),

        weight: 2.5,

        value: 50,

    };



    let player_choice =
PlayerAction::UseItem(String::from("Potion"));


    match player_choice {

        PlayerAction::Attack => println!("Player
attacks!"),

        PlayerAction::Defend => println!("Player
defends!"),

        PlayerAction::UseItem(item_name) =>
println!("Player uses {}", item_name),

    }
```

```
    println!("Item name: {}", sword.name);

}
```

In a game, Item might be a struct that stores item data, and
PlayerAction might be an enum that represents the player's
possible actions.

Exercise:

1. Create a struct called Projectile with fields for damage,
   speed, and range.
2. Create an enum called EnemyType with variants for Melee,
   Ranged, and Boss.
3. Write a function that takes a Projectile and an EnemyType
   as arguments and prints a message based on the projectile's
   damage and the enemy type.

By deeply understanding these foundational principles, we equip
ourselves with the necessary tools to build robust and efficient
game systems.

1.2 Ownership, Borrowing, and Lifetimes

Alright, let's talk about the heart and soul of Rust: ownership,
borrowing, and lifetimes. These concepts are what make Rust so
powerful and safe, especially when dealing with the complexities of
game development. We're going to break them down in a way that
feels like we're having a conversation, so you really get the ins and
outs.

Ownership: The Responsibility for Memory

At its core, ownership in Rust is about managing memory. Each
value in Rust has a variable that's its *owner*. When the owner goes

out of scope, the value is automatically dropped, which means the memory it occupies is freed. This automatic memory management is a huge advantage, as it eliminates many common memory-related bugs like dangling pointers and double frees.

Think of it this way: in a game, you might have a Player struct that contains player data. When the player leaves the game (goes out of scope), you want to ensure that the memory associated with that player is cleaned up. Rust's ownership system handles this for you.

Here's an example:

Rust

```rust
fn create_player(name: String) {

    println!("Creating player: {}", name);

    // 'name' goes out of scope here, and the
memory is freed.

}



fn main() {

    let player_name = String::from("Hero");

    create_player(player_name); // 'player_name'
is moved into 'create_player'

    // println!("{}", player_name); // This would
cause an error, as 'player_name' is no longer
valid.

}
```

In this example, player_name is moved into the create_player function. Once inside the function, name becomes the owner. When create_player finishes, name goes out of scope, and its memory is freed. Consequently, player_name is no longer valid in main.

Borrowing: Sharing Without Taking Ownership

Sometimes, you need to use data without taking ownership of it. This is where borrowing comes in. Borrowing allows you to create references to values, which let you read or modify the data without moving it.

There are two types of borrowing:

- Immutable Borrowing: You can create multiple immutable references to a value.
- Mutable Borrowing: You can create one mutable reference to a value.

Rust

```rust
fn print_player_name(player_name: &String) {

    println!("Player name: {}", player_name);

}



fn modify_player_health(player_health: &mut f32)
{

    *player_health += 10.0;

}
```

```rust
fn main() {

    let player_name = String::from("Hero");

    print_player_name(&player_name); // Immutable
borrow


    let mut player_health = 100.0;

    modify_player_health(&mut player_health); //
Mutable borrow

    println!("Player health: {}", player_health);

}
```

In this example, print_player_name takes an immutable borrow of player_name, allowing it to read the string without taking ownership. modify_player_health takes a mutable borrow of player_health, allowing it to modify the value.

Lifetimes: Ensuring References Are Valid

Lifetimes are annotations that tell the compiler how long a reference is valid. They're essential for preventing dangling references, which occur when a reference points to memory that has already been freed.

Here's a simplified example:

Rust

```rust
fn longest_name<'a>(name1: &'a String, name2: &'a
String) -> &'a String {

    if name1.len() > name2.len() {
```

```
        name1

    } else {

        name2

    }

}


fn main() {

    let name1 = String::from("Hero");

    let name2 = String::from("Villain");


    let longest = longest_name(&name1, &name2);

    println!("Longest name: {}", longest);

}
```

In this example, 'a is a lifetime annotation that tells the compiler that the returned reference has the same lifetime as the input references. This ensures that the returned reference is always valid.

In game development, lifetimes are crucial when dealing with shared data, such as game assets or player data. They ensure that references to this data remain valid throughout the game's execution.

Exercise:

1. Write a function that takes two string slices (&str) and returns the longer one.

2. Create a struct called GameAsset with a String field for the asset's name. Write a function that takes a reference to a GameAsset and prints its name.
3. Write a function that takes a mutable reference to a vector of integers (&mut Vec<i32>) and adds a new element to the vector.

By understanding ownership, borrowing, and lifetimes, we can write safe and efficient Rust code that avoids common memory-related bugs. These concepts might seem complex at first, but they become intuitive with practice. And in the context of game development, they are invaluable.

1.3 Unsafe Rust and Its Applications

Let's talk about something that can sound a bit intimidating at first: unsafe Rust. Now, the name itself suggests a level of caution, and that's absolutely warranted. However, it's also a powerful tool that, when used correctly, can unlock performance and capabilities that aren't possible with safe Rust alone.

When we talk about unsafe Rust, we're talking about bypassing some of the safety guarantees that Rust normally provides. This means we're taking on the responsibility of ensuring memory safety and avoiding undefined behavior. It's a bit like driving a high-performance race car; you get incredible speed, but you have to be extra careful.

When and Why Unsafe?

So, why would we ever want to use unsafe Rust? There are a few key scenarios:

- Interacting with C Libraries: Many existing libraries, especially in game development, are written in C. To use them from Rust, we need to interact with their C APIs, which often involves raw pointers and memory manipulation.

- Low-Level Memory Manipulation: Sometimes, we need to perform operations that Rust's safe abstraction doesn't allow, such as directly manipulating memory addresses or performing bitwise operations.
- Performance Optimization: In performance-critical sections of our code, unsafe Rust can allow us to bypass certain safety checks and achieve significant speedups. This is particularly relevant in game development, where real-time performance is essential.

Pointers and Raw Memory: Direct Access

One of the primary tools in unsafe Rust is raw pointers. Unlike Rust's safe references, raw pointers don't have lifetime guarantees or borrowing rules. They give us direct access to memory addresses.

Here's a simple example:

Rust

```
fn main() {

    let mut number = 10;

    let ptr = &mut number as *mut i32; // Create
a raw mutable pointer.


    unsafe {

        *ptr += 5; // Dereference the pointer and
modify the value.

        println!("Number: {}", *ptr);
```

```
        }

}
```

In this example, we create a raw mutable pointer to the number variable. Inside the unsafe block, we dereference the pointer and modify the value. This allows us to directly manipulate the value stored at the memory address pointed to by ptr.

In a game context, you might use raw pointers when interacting with a graphics API that requires direct memory access to pixel data or vertex buffers.

External Functions: Bridging the Gap

Another common use case for unsafe Rust is calling functions written in other languages, such as C. We use the extern keyword to declare these external functions and then call them from within an unsafe block.

```rust
Rust

extern "C" {

    fn my_c_function(x: i32) -> i32;

}


fn main() {

    unsafe {

        let result = my_c_function(20);

        println!("Result from C: {}", result);

    }
```

```
}
```

In this example, we declare an external C function called my_c_function and then call it from within an unsafe block. This allows us to use existing C libraries in our Rust code.

In game development, you might use this to integrate with a physics engine or a graphics library written in C.

Safety Considerations: The Responsibility

It's crucial to understand that unsafe Rust comes with significant responsibility. When you use unsafe code, you're essentially telling the compiler, "I know what I'm doing, and I'll make sure this is safe." If you make a mistake, you can introduce memory safety issues, data races, or undefined behavior.

Here are a few guidelines for using unsafe Rust:

- Minimize Unsafe Blocks: Keep your unsafe blocks as small as possible.
- Document Unsafe Code: Clearly document why you're using unsafe code and what invariants you're maintaining.
- Use Safe Abstractions: If possible, wrap unsafe code in safe abstractions to provide a safe interface to the rest of your code.
- Thorough Testing: Carefully test your unsafe code to ensure it's correct and safe.

Exercise:

1. Write a function that takes a raw pointer to an integer and increments the value at that address.
2. Write a simple C function that takes an integer as input and returns its square. Then, call this function from Rust using extern "C".
3. Research and describe a real world game development situation where unsafe rust would be beneficial.

Unsafe Rust is a powerful tool, but it's essential to use it judiciously and with a clear understanding of the risks. By following best practices and carefully documenting our unsafe code, we can leverage its power while minimizing the potential for errors.

1.4 Concurrency Patterns in Rust

Let's talk about concurrency in Rust. This is a big deal, especially in game development, where we often have multiple things happening at once. Think about it: you've got rendering, physics, audio, input handling, and game logic all running, ideally without stepping on each other's toes. Rust's concurrency model is designed to make this complex orchestration safe and efficient.

When we say "concurrency," we're not necessarily talking about parallelism (running things *simultaneously* on multiple cores). Concurrency is about structuring your program so that multiple tasks can *progress* independently, even if they're not all running at the exact same moment. Rust gives us tools to manage this complexity, and it does so with a focus on safety.

Threads and Message Passing: Independent Execution

One of the fundamental ways to achieve concurrency is by using threads. A thread is an independent execution context, allowing us to run code concurrently. Rust's standard library provides the std::thread module for creating and managing threads.

Communication between threads is often done through message passing. Rust's channels, provided by the std::sync::mpsc module, make this safe and efficient.

Here's a basic example:

Rust

```rust
use std::thread;

use std::sync::mpsc;


fn main() {

    let (tx, rx) = mpsc::channel();


    thread::spawn(move || {

        let message = String::from("Hello from thread!");

        tx.send(message).unwrap();

    });


    let received = rx.recv().unwrap();

    println!("Received: {}", received);

}
```

In this example, we create a channel using mpsc::channel(). We then spawn a new thread that sends a message through the channel. The main thread receives the message and prints it.

In a game, we might use threads to offload heavy computations, such as physics simulations or asset loading, to separate cores, keeping the main game loop responsive. Message passing allows these threads to communicate results or updates back to the main thread.

Mutexes and Locks: Protecting Shared Data

When multiple threads need to access shared data, we need to ensure that they don't interfere with each other. This is where mutexes (mutual exclusion locks) come in. A mutex allows only one thread to access the shared data at a time, preventing race conditions.

Rust's std::sync::Mutex provides a safe way to use mutexes.

```rust
use std::sync::Mutex;

use std::thread;

use std::sync::Arc;


fn main() {

    let counter = Arc::new(Mutex::new(0));

    let mut handles = vec![];


    for _ in 0..10 {

        let counter = Arc::clone(&counter);

        let handle = thread::spawn(move || {

            let mut num =
counter.lock().unwrap();

            *num += 1;

        });
```

```
        handles.push(handle);

    }



    for handle in handles {

        handle.join().unwrap();

    }



    println!("Counter: {}",
*counter.lock().unwrap());

}
```

In this example, we use[1] an Arc<Mutex<i32>> to share a counter between multiple threads. Each thread locks the mutex, increments the counter, and then unlocks the mutex. This ensures that the counter is updated correctly, even with multiple threads accessing it.

In a game context, a mutex might be used to protect shared game state, such as player positions or game resources, from concurrent modifications.

Atomic Operations: Lock-Free Concurrency

For simple operations, such as incrementing a counter or setting a flag, we can use atomic operations. Atomic operations are lock-free, meaning they don't require mutexes. Rust's std::sync::atomic module provides atomic types like AtomicUsize and AtomicBool.

Rust

```rust
use std::sync::atomic::{AtomicUsize, Ordering};

use std::thread;

use std::sync::Arc;


fn main() {

    let counter = Arc::new(AtomicUsize::new(0));

    let mut handles = vec![];


    for _ in 0..10 {

        let counter = Arc::clone(&counter);

        let handle = thread::spawn(move || {

            counter.fetch_add(1,
Ordering::SeqCst);

        });

        handles.push(handle);

    }


    for handle in handles {

        handle.join().unwrap();

    }
```

```
    println!("Counter: {}",
counter.load(Ordering::SeqCst));

}
```

In this example, we use an AtomicUsize to increment a counter. fetch_add performs an atomic addition, ensuring that the counter is updated correctly without requiring a mutex.

In a game, atomic operations might be used to update simple shared state, such as a frame counter or a shared resource count.

Exercise:

1. Write a program that spawns multiple threads to calculate the sum of a large array of numbers. Use message passing to send the partial sums back to the main thread.
2. Create a shared resource that multiple threads can access. Use a mutex to protect the resource from concurrent modifications.
3. Write a program that uses atomic operations to count the number of times a shared flag is set by multiple threads.

Rust's concurrency model provides powerful tools for managing complex concurrent tasks. By using threads, message passing, mutexes, and atomic operations, we can write safe and efficient concurrent code for our games.

1.5 Idiomatic and Efficient Rust Code

Let's talk about writing Rust code that's not just functional, but also feels natural and performs well. This is about more than just making the compiler happy; it's about writing code that's easy to read, maintain, and fast. In the world of game development, where performance is often critical, this becomes especially important.

When we say "idiomatic Rust," we're talking about writing code that follows the established conventions and best practices of the Rust community. It's about using the language features in the way they were intended, and it often leads to code that's more concise and expressive. When we talk about "efficient Rust," we're talking about writing code that minimizes resource usage and runs quickly.

Using Iterators and Closures: Concise and Powerful

Iterators and closures are two of Rust's most powerful features. They allow us to write concise and expressive code that performs well.

Iterators provide a way to process a sequence of values without explicitly writing loops. They're lazy, meaning they only compute values when needed, which can save resources.

Closures are anonymous functions that can capture variables from their surrounding scope. They're incredibly flexible and can be used in a variety of contexts.

Here's an example:

Rust

```rust
fn main() {

    let numbers = vec![1, 2, 3, 4, 5];



    let even_squares: Vec<i32> = numbers
```

```
    .iter()

    .filter(|&x| x % 2 == 0)

    .map(|&x| x * x)

    .collect();


    println!("Even squares: {:?}", even_squares);


}
```

In this example, we use iterators and closures to filter the numbers vector, keeping only the even numbers, and then square them. This code is concise, readable, and efficient.

In a game context, we might use iterators to process lists of game objects or to perform calculations on large datasets. Closures can be used to define custom logic for event handlers or game logic.

Avoiding Unnecessary Allocations: Performance Matters

Memory allocations can be expensive, especially in performance-critical code. Rust's ownership and borrowing system helps us minimize allocations, but we can also use techniques like reusing buffers and pre-allocating memory.

Here's an example:

```rust
Rust

fn process_data(data: &[i32], output: &mut
Vec<i32>) {

    output.clear(); // Reuse the existing vector.

    for &x in data {

        if x > 10 {

            output.push(x * 2);

        }

    }

}



fn main() {

    let data = vec![5, 12, 8, 15, 20];
```

```rust
    let mut result = Vec::new();

    process_data(&data, &mut result);

    println!("Result: {:?}", result);

}
```

In this example, we reuse the result vector by clearing it before processing the data. This avoids unnecessary allocations and improves performance.

In a game, we might reuse buffers for rendering or physics calculations to minimize memory allocations and reduce garbage collection overhead.

Profiling and Benchmarking: Measuring Performance

To write efficient code, we need to be able to measure its performance. Rust provides tools for profiling and benchmarking.

Profiling allows us to identify performance bottlenecks in our code. Benchmarking allows us to measure the performance of specific code snippets and compare different implementations.

Here's a basic benchmarking example using the criterion crate:

Rust

```rust
use criterion::{criterion_group, criterion_main,
Criterion};
```

```rust
fn fibonacci(n: u64) -> u64 {

    match n {

        0 => 1,

        1 => 1,

        n => fibonacci(n - 1) + fibonacci(n - 2),

    }

}


fn criterion_benchmark(c: &mut Criterion) {

    c.bench_function("fibonacci 20", |b|
b.iter(|| fibonacci(20)));

}
```

```
criterion_group!(benches, criterion_benchmark);


criterion_main!(benches);
```

In this example, we use the criterion crate to benchmark the fibonacci function. This allows us to measure its performance and identify potential areas for optimization.

In game development, profiling and benchmarking are essential for identifying and addressing performance bottlenecks in our game's code.

Exercise:

1. Write a function that takes a vector of strings and returns a new vector containing the lengths of each string. Use iterators and closures.
2. Write a function that processes a large dataset and reuses a buffer to minimize memory allocations.
3. Use the criterion crate to benchmark two different implementations of a function and compare their performance.

By writing idiomatic and efficient Rust code, we can create games that are not only functional but also performant and maintainable. This requires a deep understanding of Rust's features and a focus on best practices.

Chapter 2: Architectural Patterns for Game Development

Alright, let's move on to something that can really change the way you think about game development: architectural patterns. We're going to talk about how to structure our game code so it's not only efficient and fast but also maintainable and scalable. Specifically, we'll focus on the Entity-Component-System (ECS) and Data-Oriented Design (DOD). These patterns are like blueprints for building robust and high-performance game architectures in Rust.

2.1 Introduction to Entity-Component-System (ECS)

Let's really dig into the Entity-Component-System (ECS) pattern. This is a game-changer for how you structure your game code, particularly when you're dealing with a large and varied collection of game objects.[1] Imagine you're building a complex game, maybe an RPG or a simulation, and you need to manage players, enemies, items, environmental objects, and so on. If you try to manage all these objects using traditional object-oriented programming with deep inheritance hierarchies, you'll quickly find yourself in a maintenance nightmare. ECS provides a much cleaner and more flexible approach.[2]

The core idea behind ECS is to break down game objects into three fundamental concepts: Entities, Components, and Systems.

Entities: The Identifiers

An Entity, at its simplest, is just an ID. It's a unique identifier that represents a "thing" in your game.[3] Think of it like a label or a tag. An Entity by itself carries no data or behavior. It's just a way to refer to something. In practice, Entities are often represented by simple integer values, such as u32.

Here's a basic way to represent entities in Rust:

```Rust
type Entity = u32;


struct World {

    next_entity_id: Entity,

}


impl World {

    fn new() -> World {

        World { next_entity_id: 0 }

    }


    fn create_entity(&mut self) -> Entity {

        let entity = self.next_entity_id;

        self.next_entity_id += 1;

        entity

    }

}
```

```
fn main() {

    let mut world = World::new();

    let player_entity = world.create_entity();

    let enemy_entity = world.create_entity();


    println!("Player Entity: {}", player_entity);

    println!("Enemy Entity: {}", enemy_entity);

}
```

In this snippet, we use a World struct to manage our entities. The create_entity method generates a new unique Entity ID. So the Entity represents a player or an enemy, for example. In and of itself the entity represents "something exists", and nothing else.

Components: The Data

Components are the data containers. They hold the properties of an Entity. Think of them as the attributes that describe an Entity. Examples of Components might include:

- Position: Stores the x, y, and z coordinates of an Entity.
- Velocity: Stores the speed and direction of an Entity's movement.
- Health: Stores the current health of an Entity.
- Appearance: Stores information about how an Entity looks.
- Inventory: a list of items a character carries.

Components are designed to be simple data structures, ideally containing only data and no behavior. This separation of data from logic is crucial in ECS.

Here's an example with rust:

```rust
Rust

#[derive(Debug, Clone)]

struct Position {

    x: f32,

    y: f32,

}


#[derive(Debug, Clone)]

struct Health {

    value: i32,

}
```

Now we have simple data structs that can represent the properties of any entity that will need them.

Systems: The Logic

Systems are the logic processors. They operate on Entities that have specific Components.[4] Think of them as the functions that manipulate the data stored in Components. A System might, for example:

- Update the Position Component based on the Velocity Component.
- Reduce the Health Component when an Entity takes damage.

- Render the Appearance Component to display an Entity on the screen.

Here's an Example:

```rust
Rust

use std::collections::HashMap;



// Previous position and health component structs
remain.



struct World {

    positions: HashMap<Entity, Position>,

    healths: HashMap<Entity, Health>,

    next_entity_id: Entity,

}



impl World {

    //New Functionalities added

    fn new() -> World {

        World {

            positions: HashMap::new(),

            healths: HashMap::new(),
```

```rust
            next_entity_id: 0,

        }

    }


    fn create_entity(&mut self) -> Entity {

        let entity = self.next_entity_id;

        self.next_entity_id += 1;

        entity

    }


    fn add_position(&mut self, entity: Entity,
position: Position) {

        self.positions.insert(entity, position);

    }


    fn add_health(&mut self, entity: Entity,
health: Health) {

        self.healths.insert(entity, health);

    }

    //These are systems:

    fn update_positions(&mut self) {
```

```
        for position in
self.positions.values_mut() {

            position.x += 1.0;

        }

    }


    fn process_health(&mut self) {

        for (entity, health) in
self.healths.iter_mut() {

            if health.value <= 0 {

                println!("Entity {} is dead!",
entity);

            }

        }

    }

}
```

This demonstrates the separation of logic from data. The update_positions and process_health functions represent systems that operate on entities with position and health components.

The Advantages of ECS

Using ECS offers several significant advantages:

- Composition Over Inheritance: ECS promotes composition, allowing you to create complex game objects by combining simple Components.[5]

- Decoupling: ECS decouples data from logic, making your code more modular and maintainable.[6]
- Flexibility: ECS makes it easy to add or remove Components and Systems, allowing you to easily modify your game's behavior.
- Data-Oriented Design (DOD): ECS naturally lends itself to DOD, which can lead to significant performance improvements.

Exercise:

1. Create Components for velocity (x,y) and for player names.
2. Add a system, that updates the position component based on the velocity component.
3. Add a system that will print out the names of all the players.

This example illustrates how ECS separates data and logic. This separation is what gives the ECS structure its power.

2.2 Data-Oriented Design (DOD)

Let's switch gears and talk about Data-Oriented Design (DOD). While Entity-Component-System (ECS) helps us structure our game's logic and data, DOD focuses on how we organize and access that data for optimal performance. You know, making sure our games run smoothly, especially when we're dealing with a lot of moving parts.

In game development, we're constantly dealing with large amounts of data. Think about it: player positions, enemy AI, particle effects, terrain data—the list goes on. The way we lay out this data in memory can have a huge impact on our game's performance. DOD provides a set of principles and techniques to help us structure our data for maximum efficiency.

The Importance of Cache Coherency

Before we get into the specifics of DOD, let's talk about cache coherency. Modern CPUs have multiple levels of cache, which are small, fast memory stores that hold frequently accessed data. When the CPU needs to access data, it first checks the cache. If the data is in the cache (a cache hit), it can access it very quickly. If the data is not in the cache (a cache miss), the CPU has to fetch it from main memory, which is much slower.

The key to good performance is to minimize cache misses. And that's where DOD comes in.

Structure of Arrays (SOA): Organizing Data for Efficiency

One of the core principles of DOD is the Structure of Arrays (SOA). Instead of storing data as an array of structs (AOS), we store it as a struct of arrays.

Let's illustrate with an example. Imagine we have a large number of game objects, each with a position and a velocity.

Array of Structs (AOS):

```Rust
struct GameObject {

    position_x: f32,

    position_y: f32,

    velocity_x: f32,

    velocity_y: f32,

}
```

```rust
let game_objects: Vec<GameObject> = vec![/* ...
*/];
```

Structure of Arrays (SOA):

```rust
Rust

struct Positions {

    x: Vec<f32>,

    y: Vec<f32>,

}


struct Velocities {

    x: Vec<f32>,

    y: Vec<f32>,

}


struct GameData {

    positions: Positions,

    velocities: Velocities,

}


let game_data: GameData = GameData {

    positions: Positions {
```

```rust
        x: vec![/* ... */],

        y: vec![/* ... */],

    },

    velocities: Velocities {

        x: vec![/* ... */],

        y: vec![/* ... */],

    },

};
```

In the AOS approach, the position and velocity data for each game object are stored together in memory. This means that when we iterate over the game_objects vector, we're jumping around in memory, which can lead to cache misses.

In the SOA approach, the position data is stored separately from the velocity data. This means that when we iterate over the positions.x vector, we're accessing contiguous memory, which is much more cache-friendly.

Here's an example showing how we would update the position in SOA:

Rust

```rust
fn update_positions(positions: &mut Positions,
velocities: &Velocities) {

    for i in 0..positions.x.len() {

        positions.x[i] += velocities.x[i];

        positions.y[i] += velocities.y[i];
```

```
    }

}
```

Data Locality: Keeping Related Data Close

Another key principle of DOD is data locality. We want to keep related data close together in memory to minimize cache misses. This means not only using SOA but also organizing our data so that frequently accessed data is stored contiguously.

For example, if we have a large terrain dataset, we might want to store the terrain height data in a contiguous block of memory. This would allow us to efficiently access the height data for nearby terrain tiles.

Data Transformation: Processing Data Efficiently

DOD also emphasizes processing data efficiently. This often involves using vectorized operations, which allow us to perform the same operation on multiple data elements at once.

Modern CPUs have SIMD (Single Instruction, Multiple Data) instructions, which allow us to perform vectorized operations. Rust provides libraries like packed_simd and std::simd to work with SIMD instructions.

Here's a simple example using packed_simd:

```rust
Rust


use packed_simd::f32x4;



fn add_vectors(a: &[f32], b: &[f32], result: &mut
[f32]) {

    for i in (0..a.len()).step_by(4) {
```

```rust
        let a_vec =
f32x4::from_slice_unaligned(&a[i..]);

        let b_vec =
f32x4::from_slice_unaligned(&b[i..]);

        let result_vec = a_vec + b_vec;

        result_vec.write_to_slice_unaligned(&mut
result[i..]);

    }

}
```

In this example, we use f32x4 to add four floating-point numbers at once. This can significantly improve performance for operations that involve large amounts of data.

Exercise:

1. Create a struct of arrays to store the position and color data for a large number of particles.
2. Write a function that updates the position of the particles using vectorized operations.
3. Research and describe a game development situation where data locality would be highly beneficial.

By embracing DOD principles, we can write game code that not only runs faster but also makes better use of modern CPU architectures.

2.3 Implementing Architectural Patterns in Rust

Let's get practical and talk about how we can actually implement these architectural patterns, ECS and DOD, in Rust. You know, taking the theory and turning it into real, working code. Rust's features make it a fantastic language for this, giving us the tools to build efficient and maintainable game architectures.

Implementing ECS in Rust: Building the Core

When we implement ECS in Rust, we're essentially creating a data management system. We need to handle entities, components, and systems, and we want to do it in a way that's both fast and flexible.

First, let's look at how we can represent entities and components. We'll use a simple Entity type and structs for our components.

```rust
Rust

type Entity = u32;


#[derive(Debug, Clone)]

struct Position {

    x: f32,

    y: f32,

}


#[derive(Debug, Clone)]

struct Velocity {

    dx: f32,

    dy: f32,

}
```

Next, we need a way to store and manage our components. We can use HashMaps for this, where the keys are entities and the values are components.

Rust

```rust
use std::collections::HashMap;


struct World {

    positions: HashMap<Entity, Position>,

    velocities: HashMap<Entity, Velocity>,

    next_entity_id: Entity,

}


impl World {

    fn new() -> World {

        World {

            positions: HashMap::new(),

            velocities: HashMap::new(),

            next_entity_id: 0,

        }

    }
```

```rust
    fn create_entity(&mut self) -> Entity {

        let entity = self.next_entity_id;

        self.next_entity_id += 1;

        entity

    }



    fn add_position(&mut self, entity: Entity,
position: Position) {

        self.positions.insert(entity, position);

    }



    fn add_velocity(&mut self, entity: Entity,
velocity: Velocity) {

        self.velocities.insert(entity, velocity);

    }

}
```

Now, let's create a system that updates positions based on velocities.

Rust

```rust
impl World {

    fn update_positions(&mut self) {
```

```rust
        for (entity, velocity) in
self.velocities.iter() {

            if let Some(position) =
self.positions.get_mut(entity) {

                position.x += velocity.dx;

                position.y += velocity.dy;

            }

        }

    }

}
```

This simple example shows how we can create entities, add components, and implement systems in Rust.

Implementing DOD in Rust: Optimizing Data Layout

When we implement DOD in Rust, we're focusing on how we lay out our data in memory. We want to use techniques like Structure of Arrays (SOA) to improve cache coherency.

Let's re-work the previous example to use SOA:

```rust
Rust

struct Positions {

    x: Vec<f32>,

    y: Vec<f32>,

}
```

```rust
struct Velocities {

    dx: Vec<f32>,

    dy: Vec<f32>,

}


struct GameData {

    positions: Positions,

    velocities: Velocities,

    entity_map: HashMap<Entity, usize>,

    next_entity_id: Entity,

}


impl GameData {

    fn new() -> GameData {

        GameData {

            positions: Positions {

                x: Vec::new(),

                y: Vec::new(),

            },

            velocities: Velocities {
```

```rust
            dx: Vec::new(),

            dy: Vec::new(),

        },

        entity_map: HashMap::new(),

        next_entity_id: 0,

    }

}


fn create_entity(&mut self) -> Entity {

    let entity = self.next_entity_id;

    self.next_entity_id += 1;

    self.entity_map.insert(entity,
self.positions.x.len());

    self.positions.x.push(0.0);

    self.positions.y.push(0.0);

    self.velocities.dx.push(0.0);

    self.velocities.dy.push(0.0);

    entity

}


fn update_positions(&mut self) {
```

```
for i in 0..self.positions.x.len() {

    self.positions.x[i] +=
self.velocities.dx[i];

    self.positions.y[i] +=
self.velocities.dy[i];

    }

  }

}
```

In this example, we're storing positions and velocities as separate vectors, which improves cache coherency. We are also using the entity map to correctly associate the entity with its index in the vectors.

Combining ECS and DOD: Getting the Best of Both Worlds

We can combine ECS and DOD to create a powerful and efficient game architecture. We can use ECS to structure our game logic and DOD to optimize our data layout.

We might use ECS to manage our game entities and systems, and we might use DOD to store and process our component data. This allows us to take advantage of the flexibility of ECS and the performance of DOD.

Exercise:

1. Extend the ECS example to include a Renderable component and a RenderingSystem.
2. Extend the DOD example to include a Colors struct of arrays and a system that modifies the colors of entities.
3. Combine the ECS and DOD examples to create a game world that uses both patterns.

By implementing ECS and DOD in Rust, we can build games that are not only performant but also easy to develop and maintain. Rust's features make it a great language for this, giving us the tools to create robust and efficient game architectures.

2.4 Performance and Maintainability Benefits

Let's talk about why we go to all this trouble with Entity-Component-System (ECS) and Data-Oriented Design (DOD). It's not just about academic interest; there are real, tangible benefits to using these architectural patterns, especially when it comes to performance and maintainability. In game development, these two factors are absolutely crucial.

Performance: Speed Where it Counts

When we talk about performance, we're talking about how fast our game runs. And in today's demanding gaming landscape, speed is everything. Players expect smooth, responsive gameplay, even with complex graphics and physics. ECS and DOD give us the tools to achieve that.

DOD, in particular, is all about optimizing data layout for cache coherency. By using techniques like Structure of Arrays (SOA), we can significantly reduce cache misses, which translates to faster data access. Think of it like this: if you have a bunch of related data stored contiguously in memory, the CPU can grab it all at once, without having to jump around. This leads to much better performance.

Let's take a practical example. Imagine we're building a game with thousands of particles. Each particle has a position and a velocity.

If we store this data using an array of structs (AOS), like this:

Rust

```rust
struct Particle {

    position_x: f32,

    position_y: f32,

    velocity_x: f32,

    velocity_y: f32,

}
```

```rust
let particles: Vec<Particle> = vec![/* ... */];
```

When we iterate over the particles vector to update the positions, we're jumping around in memory, which can lead to cache misses.

However, if we store the data using SOA, like this:

Rust

```rust
struct ParticleData {
```

```rust
    positions_x: Vec<f32>,

    positions_y: Vec<f32>,

    velocities_x: Vec<f32>,

    velocities_y: Vec<f32>,

}



let particle_data: ParticleData = ParticleData {

    positions_x: vec![/* ... */],

    positions_y: vec![/* ... */],

    velocities_x: vec![/* ... */],

    velocities_y: vec![/* ... */],

};
```

When we update the positions, we're iterating over contiguous arrays, which is much more cache-friendly. This can lead to significant performance improvements, especially with large numbers of particles.

ECS also contributes to performance by separating data from logic. This allows us to process only the components we need, which can be more efficient than processing entire objects. For example, if we only need to update the positions of particles, we don't have to process their velocities or other data.

Maintainability: Keeping Our Code Clean

Maintainability is another crucial aspect of game development. Games are complex software projects, and they often evolve over time. We need to be able to add new features, fix bugs, and refactor code without introducing new problems.

ECS makes our code more modular and easier to understand. By separating data from logic, we can create systems that are focused on specific tasks. This makes it easier to reason about our code and to make changes without breaking other parts of the game.

For example, if we want to add a new feature that affects the health of entities, we can create a new system that operates on the Health component. We don't have to modify existing systems or add complex logic to our entities.

ECS also promotes composition over inheritance. This means we can create complex game objects by combining simple components. This makes our code more flexible and easier to extend. For example, if we want to create a new type of enemy, we can simply add the components we need, without having to create a new class or modify existing classes.

DOD also contributes to maintainability by making our code more data-driven. By focusing on how we organize and access data, we can create code that's easier to understand and optimize.

Real-World Examples

Many successful games use ECS and DOD. For example, the Unity game engine uses an ECS-like architecture, and many high-performance game engines use DOD principles.

These patterns are not just theoretical concepts; they're practical tools that can help us build better games.

Exercise:

1. Write a benchmark that compares the performance of updating particle positions using AOS and SOA.
2. Create a new component and system for a game entity.
3. Research and describe a real game engine, that uses ECS or DOD, and describe its benefits.

By embracing ECS and DOD, we can build games that are not only fast and efficient but also easy to develop and maintain. These patterns give us the tools to create complex and high-performance game architectures.

Chapter 3: Memory Management and Performance Optimization

Alright, let's get into the nitty-gritty of making our games run smoothly and efficiently. We're talking about memory management and performance optimization. In game development, these are critical areas. We need to handle memory responsibly and squeeze every bit of performance out of our systems. Rust, with its focus on safety and speed, provides us with powerful tools to do just that.

3.1 Rust's Memory Management Deep Dive

Let's really get into the nuts and bolts of how Rust handles memory. This is a topic that's fundamental to understanding Rust's safety and performance, especially in the context of game development, where we need to be very mindful of resource usage. It's not just about avoiding crashes; it's about building efficient, responsive games.

Rust's memory management is unique because it doesn't rely on a garbage collector like many other languages. Instead, it uses a system of ownership, borrowing, and lifetimes to ensure memory safety at compile time. This means that many memory-related errors are caught before your game even runs, which can save you a ton of debugging time.

Ownership: The Core Concept

The concept of ownership is central to Rust's memory management. Every value in Rust has a variable that's its *owner*. There are a few rules that govern ownership:

1. Each value in Rust has a variable that's its owner.

2. There can only be one owner at a time.

3. When the owner goes out of scope, the value[1] is dropped (deallocated).

Let's look at a simple example:

Rust

```
fn main() {

    let s1 = String::from("hello");

    let s2 = s1; // s1 is moved to s2.



    // println!("{}", s1); // This would cause an error, as s1 is no longer valid.

    println!("{}", s2);

}
```

In this example, when we assign s1 to s2, we're not copying the string data. Instead, we're *moving* the ownership of the string from s1 to s2. This means that s1 is no longer valid after the assignment. This prevents a "double free" error, which can happen if two variables try to free the same memory.

In game development, this prevents us from accidentally having two parts of the code trying to modify and then deallocate the same object.

Borrowing: Sharing Without Taking Ownership

Sometimes, we need to use a value without taking ownership of it. This is where borrowing comes in. Borrowing allows us to create references to values, which let us read or modify the data without moving it.

There are two types of borrowing:

- Immutable Borrowing: You can create multiple immutable references to a value.
- Mutable Borrowing: You can create one mutable reference to a value.

Rust

```rust
fn main() {

    let s1 = String::from("hello");

    let len = calculate_length(&s1); // Immutable
borrow.


    println!("The length of '{}' is {}.", s1,
len);


    let mut s2 = String::from("hello");

    change(&mut s2); // Mutable borrow.


    println!("The string is now: {}", s2);

}


fn calculate_length(s: &String) -> usize {
```

```
    s.len()

}


fn change(s: &mut String) {

    s.push_str(", world");

}
```

In this example, calculate_length takes an immutable borrow of s1, and change takes a mutable borrow of s2. This allows us to use the data without taking ownership, which is more efficient.

In game development, this is useful when we need to pass data to functions that only need to read or modify it temporarily. For example, when rendering an object, we might pass a reference to its position data to the rendering function.

Lifetimes: Ensuring References Are Valid

Lifetimes are annotations that tell the compiler how long a reference is valid. They're essential for preventing dangling references, which occur when a reference points to memory that has already been freed.

Here's an example:

```
Rust

fn longest<'a>(x: &'a str, y: &'a str) -> &'a str
{

    if x.len() > y.len() {

        x
```

```rust
    } else {

        y

    }

}


fn main() {

    let string1 = String::from("long string is
long");

    let result;

    {

        let string2 = String::from("xyz");

        result = longest(string1.as_str(),
string2.as_str());

    }

    println!("The longest string is {}", result);

}
```

In this example, the lifetime 'a tells the compiler that the returned reference has the same lifetime as the input references. This ensures that the returned reference is always valid.

In game development, lifetimes are crucial when dealing with shared data, such as game assets or player data. They ensure that references to this data remain valid throughout the game's execution.

Smart Pointers: Managing Memory Beyond the Basics

Rust also provides smart pointers, which are data structures that act like pointers but have additional metadata and capabilities. Box<T>, Rc<T>, and Arc<T> are examples of smart pointers.

- Box<T> is used for allocating data on the heap.
- Rc<T> (reference counted) is used for sharing ownership of data in a single-threaded context.
- Arc<T> (atomic reference counted) is used for sharing ownership of data in a multi-threaded context.

Rust

```rust
use std::rc::Rc;



fn main() {

    let a = Rc::new(String::from("hello"));

    let b = Rc::clone(&a);

    let c = Rc::clone(&a);



    println!("a: {}", a);

    println!("b: {}", b);

    println!("c: {}", c);

}
```

In game development, smart pointers can be useful for managing game assets or shared resources.

Exercise:

1. Write a function that takes ownership of a String and returns its length.
2. Write a function that takes an immutable borrow of a vector of integers and returns the sum of the elements.
3. Write a function that takes a mutable borrow of a vector of integers and sorts the elements.
4. Create a situation where Arc would be beneficial, and write a small code example.

By understanding Rust's memory management, we can write safe and efficient game code that avoids common memory-related bugs. This is a crucial skill for any game developer using Rust.

3.2 Profiling and Optimizing Game Performance

Let's get down to the business of making our games run as fast as possible. In game development, performance is king. Even the most beautiful and innovative game will fall flat if it stutters or lags. That's why profiling and optimization are essential skills for any game developer. It's not just about making things "faster"; it's about understanding where the bottlenecks are and making informed decisions about how to fix them.

Profiling: Finding the Bottlenecks

Profiling is the process of measuring the performance of your code. It's like taking a detailed health check of your game, identifying the parts that are slowing things down. Rust offers a variety of tools to help us with this.

perf (Linux): If you're on Linux, perf is your best friend. It's a powerful command-line tool that can provide detailed information about CPU usage, memory access, cache misses, and more. It's especially useful for low-level profiling.

Here's a basic example of using perf to profile a Rust program:

Bash

perf record --call-graph dwarf ./your_game

perf report

This will record the program's execution and generate a report that shows where the program spends its time. The --call-graph dwarf option is particularly useful for visualizing the call stack, which can help you pinpoint the exact functions that are slow.

cargo-profiler: This Rust crate provides a simple way to profile Rust code. It's easy to integrate into your build process and can generate flame graphs, which are visual representations of the program's execution.

Here's how to use cargo-profiler:

- Add cargo-profiler to your Cargo.toml as a dev-dependency.
- Run your program with cargo profiler run.
- Open the generated flame graph in your browser.

criterion: This is a benchmarking crate that allows you to measure the performance of specific code snippets. It's great for comparing different implementations of a function and seeing which one is faster.

Rust

```rust
use criterion::{criterion_group, criterion_main,
Criterion};


fn fibonacci(n: u64) -> u64 {

    match n {

        0 => 1,

        1 => 1,

        n => fibonacci(n - 1) + fibonacci(n - 2),

    }

}



fn criterion_benchmark(c: &mut Criterion) {

    c.bench_function("fibonacci 20", |b|
b.iter(|| fibonacci(20)));

}
```

```rust
criterion_group!(benches, criterion_benchmark);

criterion_main!(benches);
```

This example benchmarks the fibonacci function, allowing you to see how long it takes to execute.

Optimization Techniques: Making Things Faster

Once you've identified the bottlenecks, it's time to optimize your code.

Here are a few techniques that can help:

- Algorithm Optimization: Sometimes, the best way to improve performance is to choose a better algorithm. For example, if you're sorting a large array, using a quicksort algorithm will be much faster than using a bubble sort.
- Data Structure Optimization: Choosing the right data structure can also make a big difference. For example, if you need to perform frequent lookups, using a HashMap will be much faster than using a Vec.
- Loop Optimization: Loops are often a source of performance bottlenecks.

Here are a few techniques to optimize loops:

- ○ Loop Unrolling: This involves manually expanding the loop to reduce the number of loop iterations.
- ○ Vectorization (SIMD): This involves using SIMD instructions to perform the same operation on multiple data elements at once. Rust provides libraries like packed_simd and std::simd to work with SIMD instructions.
- Memory Optimization: Memory allocations can be expensive.

Here are a few techniques to minimize allocations:

- ○ Object Pooling: This involves reusing objects instead of creating new ones.

- Pre-Allocation: This involves allocating memory upfront instead of dynamically allocating it during runtime.
- Structure of Arrays (SOA): As discussed previously, this can drastically improve cache coherency.
- Profiling-Driven Optimization: Don't guess where the performance bottlenecks are. Use profiling tools to identify them. And then, focus your optimization efforts on those areas.

Real-World Examples

In game development, profiling and optimization are used extensively. For example, rendering engines are often heavily optimized to achieve high frame rates. Physics engines are also optimized to perform real-time simulations.

Here's an example of loop vectorization using packed_simd:

```rust
use packed_simd::f32x4;



fn add_vectors(a: &[f32], b: &[f32], result: &mut
[f32]) {

    for i in (0..a.len()).step_by(4) {

        let a_vec =
f32x4::from_slice_unaligned(&a[i..]);

        let b_vec =
f32x4::from_slice_unaligned(&b[i..]);
```

```
    let result_vec = a_vec + b_vec;

    result_vec.write_to_slice_unaligned(&mut
result[i..]);

    }

}
```

This example uses f32x4 to add four floating-point numbers at once, which can significantly improve performance.

Exercise:

1. Profile a game loop and identify performance bottlenecks.
2. Write a function that uses object pooling to minimize memory allocations.
3. Implement a loop optimization technique.
4. Use the criterion crate to benchmark two different implementations of a function and compare their performance.
5. Create a small simulation that is then optimized using vectorization.

By mastering profiling and optimization techniques, you can build games that are not only functional but also performant and enjoyable to play.

3.3 Minimizing Memory Allocations

Let's talk about memory allocations. In the context of game development, this is a topic that can significantly impact performance. You see, allocating and deallocating memory isn't free. It takes time, and in a real-time environment like a game, those tiny delays can add up and lead to noticeable stutters or frame rate drops. Rust, with its focus on performance and control, gives us the tools to manage memory effectively and minimize unnecessary allocations.

The problem with frequent memory allocations is that they can lead to fragmentation. The operating system has to find a free block of memory large enough for your request, and if there aren't any contiguous blocks available, it has to do some shuffling around. This process takes time, and it can also lead to cache misses, which further slow things down.

Object Pooling: Reusing Objects

One effective technique for minimizing allocations is object pooling. The idea is simple: instead of creating and destroying objects repeatedly, we create a pool of objects upfront and then reuse them as needed.

Think of it like this: in a game with many projectiles, we could create a pool of projectile objects at the start of the game. Then, when a projectile is fired, we take an object from the pool, use it, and return it to the pool when it's no longer needed.

Here's an example in Rust:

```Rust
struct Projectile {
    x: f32,
    y: f32,
    active: bool,
}


struct ProjectilePool {
```

```rust
    pool: Vec<Projectile>,

    next_index: usize,

}


impl ProjectilePool {

    fn new(size: usize) -> ProjectilePool {

        let mut pool = Vec::with_capacity(size);

        for _ in 0..size {

            pool.push(Projectile {

                x: 0.0,

                y: 0.0,

                active: false,

            });

        }

        ProjectilePool {

            pool,

            next_index: 0,

        }

    }
```

```rust
    fn get_projectile(&mut self, x: f32, y: f32)
-> Option<&mut Projectile> {

        let mut attempts = 0;

        while attempts < self.pool.len() {

            let projectile = &mut
self.pool[self.next_index];

            self.next_index = (self.next_index +
1) % self.pool.len();


            if !projectile.active {

                projectile.x = x;

                projectile.y = y;

                projectile.active = true;

                return Some(projectile);

            }

            attempts += 1;

        }

        None // Pool is full

    }


    fn return_projectile(&mut self, projectile:
&mut Projectile) {
```

```
        projectile.active = false;

    }

}


fn main() {

    let mut pool = ProjectilePool::new(10);

    if let Some(projectile) =
pool.get_projectile(10.0, 20.0) {

        println!("Projectile fired at ({}, {})",
projectile.x, projectile.y);

        pool.return_projectile(projectile);

    }

}
```

In this example, we create a ProjectilePool with a fixed size. When we need a projectile, we call get_projectile, and when we're done with it, we call return_projectile. This avoids allocating and deallocating memory for each projectile.

Pre-Allocation: Reserving Memory Upfront

Another technique is pre-allocation. Instead of allocating memory as needed, we allocate it upfront. This can be useful when we know the maximum size of our data.

For example, if we're loading a large texture, we can allocate a buffer of the required size upfront and then load the texture data into it.

```rust
Rust

fn load_texture(width: usize, height: usize,
data: &[u8]) -> Vec<u8> {

    let mut texture_data =
Vec::with_capacity(width * height * 4); // 4
bytes per pixel (RGBA).

    texture_data.extend_from_slice(data);

    texture_data

}
```

In this example, we use Vec::with_capacity to allocate a buffer of the required size upfront. This avoids reallocations as we load the texture data.

Structure of Arrays (SOA): Optimizing Data Layout

We've discussed SOA earlier, but it's worth mentioning again in the context of memory allocation. By storing data as a struct of arrays, we can improve cache coherency and reduce memory fragmentation.

For example, if we have a large number of particles, we can store their positions and velocities in separate vectors.

```rust
Rust

struct ParticleData {

    positions_x: Vec<f32>,

    positions_y: Vec<f32>,

    velocities_x: Vec<f32>,
```

```
    velocities_y: Vec<f32>,

}
```

This avoids interleaving position and velocity data, which can lead to cache misses.

String Handling: Avoiding Unnecessary Copies

String handling is another area where we can minimize allocations. Rust's String type is heap-allocated, so creating and copying strings can be expensive.

We can use string slices (&str) to avoid unnecessary copies. String slices are references to a sequence of UTF-8 encoded bytes.

Rust

```rust
fn process_string(s: &str) {

    println!("Processing: {}", s);

}


fn main() {

    let s = String::from("hello");

    process_string(&s); // Pass a string slice.

}
```

In this example, we pass a string slice to process_string, which avoids copying the string data.

Exercise:

1. Implement an object pool for a game object of your choice.

2. Write a function that pre-allocates a buffer for a large dataset.
3. Rewrite a function to use string slices instead of String to avoid unnecessary copies.
4. Create a small simulation that shows the performance difference between allocating new objects every frame, and using an object pool.

By minimizing memory allocations, we can make our games run faster and smoother. This is a crucial skill for any game developer using Rust.

3.4 Maximizing Cache Efficiency

Let's talk about something that's often overlooked but incredibly important for game performance: cache efficiency. You know, making sure our game uses the CPU's cache as effectively as possible. Modern CPUs are incredibly fast, but they rely on a hierarchy of caches to keep up with the demands of our programs. If we don't structure our data and access patterns correctly, we can end up with a lot of cache misses, which can significantly slow down our games.

Think of it like this: the CPU's cache is like a small, fast memory store that holds frequently accessed data. When the CPU needs to access data, it first checks the cache. If the data is in the cache (a cache hit), it can access it very quickly. If the data is not in the cache (a cache miss), the CPU has to fetch it from main memory, which is much slower.

Understanding Cache Lines and Coherency

The cache is organized into cache lines, which are fixed-size blocks of memory. When the CPU accesses a memory address, it loads the entire cache line containing that address into the cache. This means that if we access data that's close together in memory, we're likely to get cache hits.

Cache coherency refers to the consistency of data stored in multiple caches. If multiple cores are accessing the same data, we need to ensure that they all have the most up-to-date version.

Structure of Arrays (SOA): Organizing Data for Cache Friendliness

We've discussed SOA before, but it's worth revisiting in the context of cache efficiency. By storing data as a struct of arrays, we can improve cache locality and reduce cache misses.

Let's take a practical example. Imagine we're building a game with a large number of particles. Each particle has a position and a velocity.

Array of Structs (AOS):

Rust

```rust
struct Particle {

    position_x: f32,

    position_y: f32,

    velocity_x: f32,

    velocity_y: f32,
```

```rust
}
```

```rust
let particles: Vec<Particle> = vec![/* ... */];
```

Structure of Arrays (SOA):

Rust

```rust
struct ParticleData {

    positions_x: Vec<f32>,

    positions_y: Vec<f32>,

    velocities_x: Vec<f32>,

    velocities_y: Vec<f32>,

}
```

```rust
let particle_data: ParticleData = ParticleData {
```

```
    positions_x: vec![/* ... */],

    positions_y: vec![/* ... */],

    velocities_x: vec![/* ... */],

    velocities_y: vec![/* ... */],


};
```

In the AOS approach, the position and velocity data for each particle are stored together in memory. This means that when we iterate over the particles vector, we're jumping around in memory, which can lead to cache misses.

In the SOA approach, the position data is stored separately from the velocity data. This means that when we iterate over the positions_x vector, we're accessing contiguous memory, which is much more cache-friendly.

Data Alignment: Ensuring Optimal Access

Data alignment refers to the way data is laid out in memory. Modern CPUs can access aligned data more efficiently than unaligned data.

For example, if we have a struct with a f32 field, we want to ensure that the field is aligned to a 4-byte boundary. Rust provides the #[repr(align(4))] attribute to specify the alignment of a struct.

Rust

```
#[repr(align(4))]

struct AlignedPosition {

    x: f32,

    y: f32,

}
```

This ensures that the x and y fields are aligned to 4-byte boundaries.

Cache-Friendly Data Structures

Some data structures are more cache-friendly than others. For example, arrays and vectors are generally cache-friendly because they store data contiguously in memory. Linked lists, on the other hand, are generally cache-unfriendly because they store data in scattered locations.

When choosing a data structure, it's important to consider the access patterns of your data. If you need to perform frequent random access, a hash map might be a good choice. If you need to iterate over your data sequentially, an array or vector might be a better choice.

Prefetching: Loading Data Before It's Needed

Prefetching is a technique that allows us to load data into the cache before it's needed. Modern CPUs have hardware prefetchers that automatically load data based on access patterns. We can also use software prefetching to explicitly load data into the cache.

Rust provides the std::intrinsics::prefetch_read_data and std::intrinsics::prefetch_write_data functions to perform software prefetching.

Real-World Examples

In game development, cache efficiency is crucial for rendering, physics, and AI. Rendering engines often use SOA to store vertex data, which improves cache locality. Physics engines often use spatial data structures, such as quadtrees and octrees, to improve cache efficiency.

Exercise:

1. Write a benchmark that compares the performance of iterating over an array of structs and a struct of arrays.
2. Create a data structure that's optimized for cache efficiency.
3. Write a function that uses prefetching to load data into the cache.
4. Research and describe a real game engine that uses cache friendly data structures.

By maximizing cache efficiency, we can make our games run faster and smoother. This is a crucial skill for any game developer using Rust.

Chapter 4: Rendering Techniques

Alright, let's get into the visually exciting part of game development: rendering. We're going to discuss advanced rendering concepts and how to implement them in Rust. We'll touch on shaders, materials, lighting, post-processing, and how to integrate with powerful Rust rendering libraries. This chapter is all about making your games look amazing.

4.1 Advanced Rendering Concepts: Shaders and Materials

Let's really get into the art and science of making things look good in our games. We're going to talk about shaders and materials, which are absolutely fundamental to modern rendering. Think of shaders as the programs that tell the graphics card *how* to draw things, and materials as the recipes that describe *what* those things are made of.

Shaders: Programming the Graphics Card

Shaders are small programs that run directly on the Graphics Processing Unit (GPU). This is crucial because the GPU is highly optimized for parallel processing, which is exactly what we need for rendering. Shaders allow us to manipulate the appearance of objects with incredible flexibility and precision.

There are two main types of shaders:
Vertex Shaders:

Vertex shaders are executed for each vertex in a 3D model. Their primary responsibility is to transform the vertex's position from its original coordinates (object space) to the coordinates where it will be drawn on the screen (clip space). They also often calculate other per-vertex data, such as normals (surface directions), texture coordinates, and colors, which are then passed on to the fragment shader.

Here's a breakdown of what a vertex shader typically does:

Input: Vertex attributes (position, normal, texture coordinates, color, etc.)

Processing:

- Transformations: Applying matrices (model, view, projection) to position the vertex in the scene and project it onto the screen.
- Lighting calculations: Calculating lighting contributions at each vertex (e.g., Phong lighting).
- Other manipulations: Modifying vertex colors, texture coordinates, etc.

Output: Transformed vertex position, and interpolated vertex attributes for the fragment shader.

Fragment (Pixel) Shaders:

Fragment shaders, also known as pixel shaders, are executed for each pixel (or fragment) on the screen that is covered by a rendered object. They determine the final color of that pixel. They receive interpolated data from the vertex shader and use it, along with textures, lighting information, and other inputs, to compute the pixel's color.

Here's what a fragment shader typically does:

Input: Interpolated vertex attributes (color, texture coordinates, normals), textures, lighting information, etc.

Processing:

- Texture sampling: Fetching colors from textures.
- Lighting calculations: Applying complex lighting models (e.g., Physically Based Rendering).
- Material properties: Applying material effects (e.g., reflectivity, roughness).
- Other effects: Fog, transparency, etc.

Output: The final color of the pixel.

A Simplified Shader Example (GLSL)

Shaders are usually written in a language similar to C, such as GLSL (OpenGL Shading Language) or HLSL (High-Level Shading Language). Let's look at a very basic GLSL example to get a feel for how they work:

Vertex Shader:

```
OpenGL Shading Language
```

```glsl
#version 450 core


layout (location = 0) in vec3 aPos;    // Vertex
position

layout (location = 1) in vec3 aColor;  // Vertex
color


out vec3 vertexColor; // Output to fragment
shader


uniform mat4 model;       // Model matrix

uniform mat4 view;        // View matrix

uniform mat4 projection; // Projection matrix


void main() {

    gl_Position = projection * view * model *
vec4(aPos, 1.0);

    vertexColor = aColor;

}
```

This shader takes vertex positions and colors as input, multiplies the position by transformation matrices to place it in the scene and on the screen, and passes the color to the fragment shader.

Fragment Shader:

OpenGL Shading Language

```
#version 450 core


in vec3 vertexColor;    // Color from vertex
shader

out vec4 fragColor;   // Output color


void main() {

    fragColor = vec4(vertexColor, 1.0);

}
```

This shader simply takes the color from the vertex shader and outputs it as the pixel's color.

Materials: Defining Surface Properties

Materials define how light interacts with the surface of an object. They're like the "recipe" for how an object should look. Materials can include various properties that affect the way an object reflects light, its color, and its texture.

Common material properties include:

Albedo (Base Color): The fundamental color of the surface. This is what the object looks like under direct white light.

Metallic: A value indicating how metallic the surface is. Metallic surfaces reflect light differently than non-metallic surfaces.

Roughness: A value indicating how rough or smooth the surface is. Rough surfaces scatter light in many directions, while smooth surfaces reflect light in a more specular (mirror-like) way.

Normal Map: A texture that stores surface normals. This allows us to simulate detailed surfaces without using a high number of polygons.

Emissive: A color that specifies how much light the surface emits.

Putting It Together

Shaders and materials work together to create the final appearance of an object. The shaders calculate how the object should be rendered based on the material properties, lighting conditions, and other factors.

For example, to render a shiny metal sphere, we would use a shader that calculates specular reflections based on the roughness and metallic properties of the material. We would also provide textures for the albedo color and potentially a normal map to add surface detail.

In Rust

In Rust, you don't directly write GLSL/HLSL in your Rust code. Instead, you would:

1. Write your shaders in GLSL/HLSL separately.
2. Compile those shaders (using tools provided by your rendering API) into a format the GPU understands.
3. In your Rust code, you would use a rendering library (like wgpu or rend3) to:
   - Load the compiled shaders.

- Set up the shader program.
- Pass material data (albedo, metallic, roughness, textures) to the shader as uniforms.
- Draw the object.

Exercise

1. Write a simple GLSL vertex shader that only transforms the vertex position.
2. Write a simple GLSL fragment shader that outputs a solid color.
3. Explain the difference between albedo and specular reflection.
4. Describe how a normal map can be used to add detail to a surface.
5. Research and explain how shaders are used to create realistic water rendering.

Shaders and materials are the building blocks of modern rendering. By understanding how they work, you can create visually stunning and realistic games.

4.2 Lighting and Post-Processing

Let's continue our exploration of rendering and talk about two crucial elements that drastically affect the visual quality of a game: lighting and post-processing. Lighting gives our scenes depth and realism, while post-processing adds that final layer of polish and artistic flair.

Lighting: Illuminating the Scene

Lighting is how we simulate the way light interacts with objects in our game world.[1] It's what gives objects shape, volume, and makes them feel like they're actually present in the scene. Without proper lighting, even the most detailed models can look flat and unconvincing.

There are several types of light sources commonly used in games:

Directional Lights:

Directional lights represent light sources that are infinitely far away, like the sun.[2] They emit parallel rays of light, meaning all objects in the scene are lit from the same direction.[3] Directional lights are efficient to calculate but lack the localized effect of other light types.

Properties:

Direction: The direction the light is shining.

Color: The color of the light.

Intensity: The brightness of the light.

Point Lights:

Point lights emit light from a single point in space, like a light bulb.[4] Light from a point light spreads out in all directions, attenuating (becoming weaker) with distance.[5] Point lights create more realistic lighting effects than directional lights but are computationally more expensive.

Properties:

Position: The position of the light source.

Color: The color of the light.

Intensity: The brightness of the light.

Attenuation: How the light intensity decreases with distance.

Spot Lights:

Spot lights are similar to point lights but emit light in a cone shape, like a flashlight.[6] They provide a focused light source with a defined direction and falloff.

Properties:

Position: The position of the light source.

Direction: The direction the light is pointing.

Color: The color of the light.

Intensity: The brightness of the light.

Attenuation: How the light intensity decreases with distance.

Cone Angle: The width of the light cone.

Cone Falloff: How smoothly the light transitions from the center to the edge of the cone.

Lighting Models: Calculating Light Interaction

To determine how light affects the color of a surface, we use lighting models. These models simulate the way light reflects off different materials.[7]

Phong Lighting:

Phong lighting is a simple and widely used lighting model. It calculates the final color of a pixel based on three components:

- Ambient light: A constant amount of light that illuminates all surfaces equally.[8]
- Diffuse light: The light reflected from a surface that depends on the angle between the light source and the surface normal (the direction the surface is facing).
- Specular light: The bright highlight that occurs when light reflects off a shiny surface.[9]

Phong lighting is relatively inexpensive to calculate but can produce unrealistic results for certain materials.

Physically Based Rendering (PBR):

PBR is a more advanced lighting model that aims to simulate the way light interacts with materials in the real world.[10] It uses physically accurate properties like roughness and metallic to produce more realistic lighting effects. PBR is more computationally expensive than Phong lighting but results in significantly improved visual quality.

Post-Processing: The Finishing Touches

Post-processing effects are applied to the entire rendered image after the scene has been drawn.[11] They're like adding filters to a photograph, enhancing the visual style and creating cinematic effects.

Common post-processing effects include:

Bloom:

Bloom creates a glowing effect around bright objects, simulating the way light scatters in the eye or a camera lens.[12] It adds a sense of intensity and can make scenes feel more vibrant.

Depth of Field (DOF):

DOF simulates the way a camera lens focuses on a specific distance, blurring objects that are closer or farther away.[13] It adds a sense of realism and can draw the viewer's attention to specific parts of the scene.

Motion Blur:

Motion blur simulates the blurring of moving objects, making them appear smoother and faster.[14] It adds a sense of speed and dynamism to action scenes.

Color Grading:

Color grading allows you to adjust the overall color and tone of the image, creating specific moods or artistic styles.[15] It's similar to applying color filters in photo editing.

Implementing Lighting and Post-Processing

Lighting calculations are typically performed in the fragment shader, where we have access to per-pixel information.[16] Post-processing effects are also usually implemented using fragment shaders, processing the rendered image as a texture.

Example: Basic Phong Lighting

Here's a simplified GLSL fragment shader example that implements basic Phong lighting:

```
OpenGL Shading Language

#version 450 core



in vec3 FragPos;
```

```glsl
in vec3 Normal;

out vec4 FragColor;

uniform vec3 lightPos;

uniform vec3 lightColor;

uniform vec3 viewPos;

uniform vec3 objectColor;

void main() {
    // Ambient
    float ambientStrength = 0.1;
    vec3 ambient = ambientStrength * lightColor;


    // Diffuse
    vec3 norm = normalize(Normal);
    vec3 lightDir = normalize(lightPos -
FragPos);
    float diff = max(dot(norm, lightDir), 0.0);
    vec3 diffuse = diff * lightColor;
```

```
// Specular

float specularStrength = 0.5;

vec3 viewDir = normalize(viewPos - FragPos);

vec3 reflectDir = reflect(-lightDir, norm);

float spec = pow(max(dot(viewDir,
reflectDir), 0.0), 32);

vec3 specular = specularStrength * spec *
lightColor;


FragColor = vec4(ambient + diffuse +
specular, 1.0) * vec4(objectColor, 1.0);

}
```

This shader calculates the ambient, diffuse, and specular components of lighting and combines them to determine the final pixel color.[17]

Exercise

1. Explain the difference between a directional light and a point light.
2. Describe how the Phong lighting model works.
3. Choose three post-processing effects and explain how they enhance the visual quality of a game.
4. Write a fragment shader that implements a simple bloom effect.
5. Research and explain how deferred rendering can be used to improve the performance of lighting calculations.

Lighting and post-processing are essential tools for creating visually compelling and immersive games. By understanding these techniques, you can elevate your game's graphics to the next level.

4.3 Integration with Rust Rendering Libraries (wgpu, rend3)

Let's talk about how to actually get those beautiful rendering techniques we discussed working in Rust. We don't want to reinvent the wheel, right? Thankfully, Rust has some fantastic rendering libraries that handle the heavy lifting of talking to the GPU. We'll focus on two popular and powerful options: wgpu and rend3.

wgpu: The Cross-Platform GPU Abstraction

wgpu is a cross-platform, safe, and portable GPU abstraction library developed by the Mozilla team. It's designed to expose modern GPU features in a way that's consistent across different platforms, including desktop (Windows, macOS, Linux), web (via WebGPU), and mobile (Android, iOS).

Think of wgpu as a translator. It allows your Rust code to speak the language of the GPU without you having to worry about the specifics of each operating system or graphics API (like DirectX, Vulkan, or Metal). This makes it a great choice for writing portable and high-performance graphics applications.

Here's a breakdown of what wgpu provides:

- Platform Abstraction: It handles the differences between various graphics APIs and operating systems, giving you a unified API to work with.
- Safety: It's written in Rust, so you get all the safety benefits of the language, such as memory safety and thread safety.

- Modern GPU Features: It exposes modern GPU capabilities, such as compute shaders, indirect drawing, and bind groups.
- WebGPU Support: It's the library that backs WebGPU, meaning your Rust rendering code can run in the browser.

A Simplified wgpu **Example**

Let's look at a very basic wgpu example to get a sense of how it works. This example sets up a minimal rendering pipeline to draw a triangle.

```rust
Rust

use wgpu::*;

use winit::{

    event::*,

    event_loop::{ControlFlow, EventLoop},

    window::WindowBuilder,

};



async fn run() {

    // 1. Instance: The entry point to wgpu.

    let instance =
Instance::new(InstanceDescriptor::default());



    // 2. Adapter: Represents a physical GPU.
```

```rust
    let adapter =
instance.request_adapter(&RequestAdapterOptions::
default()).await.unwrap();


    // 3. Device and Queue: The logical device
and command queue.

    let (device, queue) = adapter

        .request_device(

            &DeviceDescriptor {

                label: None,

                features: Features::empty(),

                limits: Limits::default(),

            },

            None,

        )

        .await

        .unwrap();



    // 4. Window and Surface: Create a window and
the surface to render to.

    let event_loop = EventLoop::new();

    let window =
WindowBuilder::new().build(&event_loop).unwrap();
```

```rust
    let surface = unsafe {
instance.create_surface(&window) }.unwrap();


    // 5. Surface Configuration: Configure the
surface for rendering.

    let surface_caps =
surface.get_capabilities(&adapter);

    let surface_format = surface_caps

        .formats

        .iter()

        .copied()

        .find(|f| f.is_srgb())

        .unwrap_or(surface_caps.formats[0]);


    let config = SurfaceConfiguration {

        usage: SurfaceUsages::RENDER_ATTACHMENT,

        format: surface_format,

        width: window.inner_size().width,

        height: window.inner_size().height,

        present_mode: PresentMode::Fifo,

        alpha_mode: surface_caps.alpha_modes[0],

        view_formats: vec![],
```

```
    };

    surface.configure(&device, &config);



    // 6. Shader Modules: Load and compile the
shaders.

    let vs_module =
device.create_shader_module(ShaderModuleDescripto
r {

        label: Some("Vertex Shader"),

        source: ShaderSource::Wgsl(

            "

            @vertex

            fn vs_main(@builtin(vertex_index)
in_vertex_index: u32) -> @builtin(position)
vec4<f32> {

                let positions = array(

                    vec2f(-0.5, -0.5),

                    vec2f(0.5, -0.5),

                    vec2f(0.0, 0.5)

                );

                let position =
positions[in_vertex_index];

                return vec4f(position, 0.0, 1.0);
```

```rust
        }
        "
        .into(),
    ),
});


    let fs_module =
device.create_shader_module(ShaderModuleDescripto
r {
        label: Some("Fragment Shader"),
        source: ShaderSource::Wgsl(
            "
            @fragment
            fn fs_main() -> @location(0)
vec4<f32> {
                return vec4f(1.0, 0.0, 0.0, 1.0);
// Red color
            }
            "
            .into(),
        ),
    });
```

```rust
    // 7. Render Pipeline: Create the render
pipeline.

    let render_pipeline_layout =
device.create_pipeline_layout(&PipelineLayoutDesc
riptor {

        label: Some("Render Pipeline Layout"),

        bind_group_layouts: &[],

        push_constant_ranges: &[],

    });


    let render_pipeline =
device.create_render_pipeline(&RenderPipelineDesc
riptor {

        label: Some("Render Pipeline"),

        layout: Some(&render_pipeline_layout),

        vertex: VertexState {

            module: &vs_module,

            entry_point: "vs_main",

            buffers: &[],

        },

        fragment: Some(FragmentState {

            module: &fs_module,
```

```
        entry_point: "fs_main",

        targets: &[Some(SurfaceTargetState {

            format: surface_format,

            blend: Some(BlendState::REPLACE),

            write_mask: ColorWrites::ALL,

        })],

    }),

    primitive: PrimitiveState {

        topology:
PrimitiveTopology::TRIANGLE_LIST,

        strip_index_format: None,

        front_face: FrontFace::Ccw,

        cull_mode: Some(CullMode::Back),

        polygon_mode: PolygonMode::Fill,

        unclipped_depth: false,

        conservative: false,

    },

    depth_stencil: None,

    multisample: MultisampleState {

        count: 1,

        mask: !0,
```

```rust
                alpha_to_coverage_enabled: false,

            },

            multiview: None,

        });



    // 8. Render Loop: The main loop where we
draw our scene.

    event_loop.run(move |event, _, control_flow|
match event {

        Event::WindowEvent {

            window_id,

            event: WindowEvent::Resized(size),

        } if window_id == window.id() => {

            if size.width > 0 && size.height > 0
{

                config.width = size.width;

                config.height = size.height;

                surface.configure(&device,
&config);

            }

        }

        Event::RedrawRequested(window_id) if
window_id == window.id() => {
```

```rust
        let output =
surface.get_current_texture().unwrap();

        let view = output

            .texture

.create_view(&TextureViewDescriptor::default());

        let mut encoder =
device.create_command_encoder(&CommandEncoderDesc
riptor {

            label: Some("Render Encoder"),

        });


        {

            let mut render_pass =
encoder.begin_render_pass(&RenderPassDescriptor {

                label: Some("Render Pass"),

                color_attachments:
&[Some(RenderPassColorAttachment {

                    view: &view,

                    resolve_target: None,

                    ops: Operations {

                        load:
LoadOp::Clear(Color {
```

```
                                        r: 0.1,

                                        g: 0.2,

                                        b: 0.3,

                                        a: 1.0,

                                    }),

                                store:
StoreOp::Store,

                            },

                        })],

                    depth_stencil_attachment:
None,

                });



    render_pass.set_pipeline(&render_pipeline);

                render_pass.draw(0..3, 0..1);

            }



    queue.submit(std::iter::once(encoder.finish()));

            output.present();

        }
```

```
        Event::MainEventsCleared => {

            window.request_redraw();

        }

        Event::WindowEvent {

            window_id,

            event: WindowEvent::CloseRequested,

        } if window_id == window.id() =>
*control_flow = ControlFlow::Exit,

            _ => {}

    });

}



fn main() {

    pollster::block_on(run());

}
```

This code is fairly involved, but it demonstrates the basic steps of setting up a wgpu rendering pipeline:

1. Instance: Create a wgpu::Instance.
2. Adapter: Request a wgpu::Adapter (a physical GPU).
3. Device and Queue: Request a wgpu::Device and wgpu::Queue (the logical device and command queue).
4. Window and Surface: Create a window and a surface to render to.
5. Surface Configuration: Configure the surface.

6. Shader Modules: Create wgpu::ShaderModules for the vertex and fragment shaders.
7. Render Pipeline: Create a wgpu::RenderPipeline.
8. Render Loop: The main loop where we draw our scene.

rend3: A Higher-Level Rendering Engine

rend3 is a higher-level rendering engine built on top of wgpu. It aims to provide a more user-friendly and feature-rich API for building 3D applications. rend3 handles many of the low-level details of interacting with wgpu, allowing you to focus on the game's logic and art.

rend3 offers features like:

- Scene Graph: A hierarchical structure for organizing objects in the scene.
- Material System: A flexible system for defining material properties.
- Mesh Loading: Support for loading various mesh formats.
- Camera Control: Built-in camera controllers.
- Renderer: A renderer that handles drawing objects in the scene.

Using rend3 can significantly simplify the process of setting up a rendering pipeline, especially for more complex scenes.

Choosing Between wgpu and rend3

The choice between wgpu and rend3 depends on your project's needs:

- Use wgpu if:
  - You need fine-grained control over the rendering pipeline.
  - You're targeting multiple platforms, including the web.

- You're comfortable with lower-level graphics programming.
- Use rend3 if:
  - You want a more user-friendly and feature-rich API.
  - You want to get up and running quickly.
  - You don't need the same level of control as wgpu.

Exercise

1. Explain the key differences between wgpu and rend3.
2. Describe the benefits of using a cross-platform rendering library like wgpu.
3. Modify the wgpu example to change the color of the triangle.
4. Research and describe how to load a 3D model in rend3.
5. Create a small project that uses either wgpu or rend3 to render a simple scene.

By integrating with powerful Rust rendering libraries like wgpu and rend3, you can leverage the full potential of modern GPUs and create visually stunning games.

4.4 Optimizing Rendering Pipelines

Let's discuss a critical aspect of game development: optimizing rendering pipelines. Even with powerful GPUs, inefficient rendering can lead to performance bottlenecks, causing frame rate drops and a poor player experience. Optimizing the rendering pipeline is about making smart choices about how we draw objects to the screen to minimize the work the GPU has to do.

A rendering pipeline is the sequence of steps the GPU takes to transform 3D data into the 2D image we see on the screen. It involves vertex processing, rasterization, and fragment processing.

Optimizing this pipeline is about reducing the number of draw calls, minimizing overdraw, and efficiently using GPU resources.

Here are several key techniques for optimizing rendering pipelines:

1. Batching: Reducing Draw Calls

Draw calls are commands from the CPU to the GPU to draw something. Each draw call has overhead, so reducing the number of draw calls can significantly improve performance.

Batching involves combining multiple objects with the same material and shaders into a single draw call. Instead of drawing each object individually, we send all their vertex data to the GPU at once.

For example, if you have many trees in a forest that use the same material, you can batch them together.

How it works:

Group objects by material and shader.

Store their vertex data in a single vertex buffer.

Issue a single draw call that draws all the objects.

Benefits:

Reduces CPU overhead.

Improves GPU efficiency.

Example:

Imagine drawing 100 identical cubes. Without batching, you'd make 100 draw calls. With batching, you make 1.

2. Instancing: Drawing Multiple Copies Efficiently

Instancing is a technique for drawing multiple copies of the same mesh with different transformations (position, rotation, scale) in a single draw call. This is even more efficient than batching when you have identical or very similar objects.

For example, you can use instancing to draw thousands of particles, blades of grass, or similar objects.

How it works:

Send the mesh data to the GPU once.

Send an array of transformation matrices (or other per-instance data) to the GPU.

The vertex shader uses the per-instance data to draw each copy of the mesh.

Benefits:

Extremely efficient for drawing many copies of the same mesh.

Reduces both CPU and GPU overhead.

Example:

Drawing 10,000 identical rocks. Without instancing, you might batch them, but instancing is even better because the GPU can efficiently use the instance data.

3. Level of Detail (LOD): Rendering Distant Objects Efficiently

Level of Detail (LOD) involves rendering objects with lower detail when they're far away from the camera. This reduces the number of polygons that the GPU has to process.

For example, a character model might have a high-resolution version for close-ups and a low-resolution version for when it's in the distance.

How it works:

Create multiple versions of a mesh with varying levels of detail.

Switch between these versions based on the distance from the camera.

Benefits:

Reduces the number of polygons processed.

Improves performance, especially in scenes with many objects.

Example:

A city skyline. Buildings far away are rendered with simpler models than those close to the player.

4. Frustum Culling: Avoiding Unnecessary Rendering

The view frustum is the 3D region that's visible to the camera. Frustum culling involves not rendering objects that are outside the view frustum. This prevents the GPU from wasting time processing objects that the player can't see.

How it works:

Calculate the view frustum based on the camera's position, orientation, and field of view.

Test each object against the view frustum.

Only render objects that are inside the frustum.

Benefits:

Reduces the number of objects rendered.

· Improves performance, especially in large scenes.

Example:

In an open-world game, objects behind the player are culled because they are outside the camera's view.

5. Occlusion Culling: Hiding Hidden Objects

Occlusion culling involves not rendering objects that are hidden behind other objects. This is more complex than frustum culling but can provide significant performance improvements in dense scenes.

How it works:

Use techniques like depth testing or hierarchical z-buffering to determine which objects are visible.

Don't render objects that are completely occluded.

Benefits:

Reduces overdraw (rendering pixels that will be overwritten).

Improves performance in scenes with many overlapping objects.

Example:

In a room filled with furniture, objects behind a wall are occluded and don't need to be rendered.

6. Shader Optimization: Efficient GPU Programs

Shaders are programs that run on the GPU. Optimizing shaders can significantly improve rendering performance.

Techniques:

Reduce the number of calculations in the shader.

Use simpler mathematical operations.

Minimize texture lookups.

Avoid branching (if-else statements) in shaders.

Example:

Using a simpler lighting model (like Phong) instead of a more complex one (like PBR) when performance is critical.

7. Render Target Optimization: Reducing Render Passes

A render target is a buffer where the GPU renders an image. Sometimes, rendering a scene requires multiple render passes, which can be expensive.

Techniques:

Combine render passes if possible.

Use techniques like deferred rendering to optimize lighting calculations.

Example:

Deferred rendering calculates lighting in a separate pass after the scene geometry is rendered, which can be more efficient for complex lighting scenarios.

Example: Rust and Instancing

Here's a simplified conceptual example of how instancing might be done in Rust (using a hypothetical simplified rendering API):

```rust
Rust

struct InstanceData {

    position: [f32; 3],

    rotation: [f32; 3],

    scale: [f32; 3],

}
```

```rust
fn render_objects(

    mesh: &Mesh, // Hypothetical mesh type

    instances: &[InstanceData],

    render_api: &mut RenderApi, // Hypothetical
rendering API

) {

    let instance_buffer =
render_api.create_buffer_with_data(

        instances,

        BufferUsage::VERTEX, // Hypothetical
usage flag

    );


    render_api.draw_mesh_instanced(

        mesh,
```

```
        &instance_buffer,

        instances.len() as u32,

    );

}


// In a real scenario, you'd use a library like
wgpu or rend3.
```

Exercise

1. Explain the performance benefits of batching and instancing.
2. Describe how level of detail (LOD) improves rendering performance.
3. Compare and contrast frustum culling and occlusion culling.
4. Research and describe how a real game engine uses a specific rendering optimization technique.
5. Create a small simulation that shows the performance difference between rendering many objects individually and using instancing.

By understanding and applying these optimization techniques, you can build games that are both visually stunning and performant, providing a smooth and enjoyable experience for players.

Chapter 5: Input Handling and Game Logic

This chapter is all about making your game interactive! We're going to explore how to take the raw actions of a player—button presses, mouse movements, controller inputs—and turn them into meaningful events within the game. We'll also cover the crucial topic of game logic: the rules and systems that govern how your game works, from character movement to AI behavior. Finally, we'll look at how to structure the overall flow of your game, managing transitions between menus, levels, and other states.

Think of it this way: input handling is the game's ears, listening to the player, while game logic is its brain, deciding how to react. A well-designed input system makes the game feel responsive and intuitive, while solid game logic makes it engaging and consistent. Together, they create the interactive experience that keeps players coming back for more.

Okay, let's take a deep but easy breath and talk about building a solid input system for your game. This is where we create that essential connection between the player and your game, so getting it right is super important.

5.1 Implementing Robust Input Systems

Okay, let's really break down what it takes to build a solid input system for your game. This is a super important area because it's how players connect with your game, and a good input system can make all the difference in how enjoyable it is to play.

When we talk about a "robust" input system, we're talking about one that's reliable, adaptable, and handles all the different ways players might want to control the game. It's not just about registering button presses; it's about creating a smooth, responsive, and customizable experience.

Here are the key things we need to think about:

Device Abstraction: Speaking the Player's Language

Think about the sheer variety of devices players use: keyboards, mice, gamepads, touchscreens, joysticks, and even specialized controllers. Each of these sends input to the computer in its own way. Your game's core logic shouldn't have to deal with those device-specific details.

This is where device abstraction comes in. It's like having a translator that sits between the raw input from the device and your game's code. This "translator" takes the device-specific signals and converts them into game actions.

- Game Actions: These are abstract representations of what the player wants to *do* in the game, like "jump," "fire," "move," "interact," etc. They're independent of any particular device.
- Abstraction Layer: This is the code that performs the translation. It maps raw input from different devices to the corresponding game actions.

Let's see how this works with some examples:

- If the player presses the spacebar on a keyboard, the abstraction layer says, "Okay, that means the player wants to 'jump'."
- If the player presses the "A" button on a gamepad, the abstraction layer *also* says, "Okay, that *also* means the player wants to 'jump'."

Now, your game logic only needs to listen for "jump" actions. It doesn't need to know *how* the player triggered that action.

Why is this so beneficial?

- Portability: Your game becomes much easier to adapt to different platforms (PC, consoles, mobile) and support a wider range of controllers.
- Maintainability: If you change the control scheme or need to support a new device, you only need to update the abstraction layer, not your core game logic.
- Clarity: Your game code becomes cleaner and easier to understand, because it's focused on *what* the player is doing, not *how* they're doing it.

A Conceptual Example in Rust:

```rust
Rust

use std::collections::HashMap;



// Define the actions a player can take in the game

#[derive(Debug, PartialEq, Eq, Hash, Copy, Clone)]

enum GameAction {

    Jump,

    Fire,

    MoveLeft,

    MoveRight,

    // ... other actions

}
```

```rust
// Define the different types of input events
#[derive(Debug, PartialEq, Eq, Hash, Copy,
Clone)]
enum InputEvent {
    Keyboard(KeyCode),
    Gamepad(GamepadButton),
    // ... other input events
}


// Define the different keys on a keyboard
#[derive(Debug, PartialEq, Eq, Hash, Copy,
Clone)]
enum KeyCode {
    Space,
    LeftShift,
    // ... other keys
}


// Define the different buttons on a gamepad
#[derive(Debug, PartialEq, Eq, Hash, Copy,
Clone)]
```

```rust
enum GamepadButton {

    A,

    X,

    // ... other buttons

}



struct InputManager {

    // Store the current state of keys/buttons
    (e.g., pressed or not pressed)

    key_states: HashMap<KeyCode, bool>,

    gamepad_states: HashMap<GamepadButton, bool>,

    // Store the current input mappings

    input_mappings: HashMap<InputEvent,
    GameAction>,

}



impl InputManager {

    fn new() -> Self {

        InputManager {

            key_states: HashMap::new(),

            gamepad_states: HashMap::new(),
```

```rust
            input_mappings: HashMap::new(),

    }

}



    // Set up the default input mappings

    fn set_default_mappings(&mut self) {


self.input_mappings.insert(InputEvent::Keyboard(K
eyCode::Space), GameAction::Jump);


self.input_mappings.insert(InputEvent::Gamepad(Ga
mepadButton::A), GameAction::Jump);

        // ... other default mappings

    }



    // Process a raw input event and translate it
into a GameAction

    fn process_input_event(&self, event:
InputEvent) -> Option<GameAction> {

        self.input_mappings.get(&event).copied()

    }
```

```rust
    // Simulate getting input events (in a real
game, you'd use a library)

    fn get_input_events(&self) -> Vec<InputEvent>
{
        vec![
            InputEvent::Keyboard(KeyCode::Space),

InputEvent::Gamepad(GamepadButton::A),

InputEvent::Keyboard(KeyCode::LeftShift),

        ]
    }


    // Handle all input for the current frame
    fn handle_input(&mut self) -> Vec<GameAction>
{
        let mut actions = Vec::new();


        let events = self.get_input_events(); //
Get raw input events

        for event in events {
```

```rust
            if let Some(action) =
self.process_input_event(event) {

                actions.push(action);

            }

        }


        actions

    }

}


fn main() {

    let mut input_manager = InputManager::new();

    input_manager.set_default_mappings();


    let actions = input_manager.handle_input();


    for action in actions {

        match action {

            GameAction::Jump => {

                // Handle the jump action in your
game
```

```
                println!("Player wants to
jump!");

            }

        GameAction::Fire => {

            // Handle the fire action

        }

        // ... other actions

        }

    }

}
```

This is a simplified example. A production-ready input manager would be more complex and involve interacting with operating system APIs or input libraries like SDL or winit.

Input Buffering: Catching Every Action

Players can sometimes provide input very quickly, pressing buttons or moving controls faster than your game's update loop. If you only check for input once per frame, you might miss some of these quick inputs, leading to a feeling of unresponsiveness.

Input buffering solves this problem. It's like a temporary storage where input events are held until the game is ready to process them.

- Input Buffer: A data structure (often a queue) that stores input events as they occur.
- When an input event happens (a key is pressed, a mouse button is clicked), it's added to the buffer.

- The game then processes the events from the buffer at its own pace (usually once per frame).

Why is this important?

- Responsiveness: Makes the game feel more responsive, even when players are inputting commands very rapidly.
- Consistency: Helps to ensure that input is handled consistently, regardless of frame rate variations.

A Conceptual Example in Rust:

```rust
Rust

use std::collections::VecDeque;


struct InputBuffer {

    events: VecDeque<InputEvent>, // Using a
double-ended queue

}


impl InputBuffer {

    fn new() -> Self {

        InputBuffer {

            events: VecDeque::new(),

        }

    }
```

```rust
    fn add_event(&mut self, event: InputEvent) {

        self.events.push_back(event); // Add to
the back of the queue

    }


    fn get_events(&mut self) -> Vec<InputEvent> {

        let mut processed_events = Vec::new();

        while let Some(event) =
self.events.pop_front() { // Remove from the
front

            processed_events.push(event);

        }

        processed_events

    }

}


fn main() {

    let mut input_buffer = InputBuffer::new();


    // Simulate some input events
```

```rust
input_buffer.add_event(InputEvent::Keyboard(KeyCo
de::Space));

input_buffer.add_event(InputEvent::Gamepad(Gamepa
dButton::A));

input_buffer.add_event(InputEvent::Keyboard(KeyCo
de::Space)); // Rapid press


    // Process the events (e.g., once per frame)

    let events = input_buffer.get_events();

    for event in events {

        match event {

            InputEvent::Keyboard(KeyCode::Space)
=> println!("Jump!"),

            InputEvent::Gamepad(GamepadButton::A)
=> println!("Also Jump!"),

            _ => {}

        }

    }

}
```

This example shows how an input buffer can smooth out input and prevent missed actions.

Input Polling vs. Event-Driven Input: Two Ways to Listen

There are two main strategies for how your game listens for player input:

- Input Polling: The game actively *checks* the state of input devices at regular intervals (usually every frame).

  It asks questions like:

  - "Is the spacebar currently pressed?"
  - "What's the current position of the mouse?"
  - "What's the value of the gamepad's analog stick?"
- Polling gives you a snapshot of the input device's state at the moment you check it.
- Event-Driven Input: The game reacts to *events* that are generated by the operating system or input libraries when input occurs. It's like setting up listeners that are triggered when:
  - A key is pressed or released.
  - A mouse button is clicked.
  - A gamepad button is pressed.
- Event-driven input provides immediate notification when something changes.

Comparison Table:

Feature	Input Polling	Event-Driven Input
Updates	Regularly (e.g., every frame)	Only when events occur

| Responsiveness | Can have slight delay (depends on polling rate) | Immediate response to events |

| Overhead | Constant, even if no input | Only when events occur |

| Use Cases | Continuous input, state (e.g., movement) | Discrete actions, changes (e.g., button press) |

How They're Used Together:

Game developers often combine both approaches:

- Polling: For continuous input, like character movement. You poll the keyboard or analog sticks to get the player's current direction.
- Event-Driven: For discrete actions, like jumping or firing a weapon. You use events to trigger those actions when the corresponding buttons are pressed.

Input Mapping and Rebinding: Player Control

Giving players control over their controls is essential for a good user experience and accessibility.

- Input Mapping: This is the initial assignment of game actions to specific input devices and buttons. For example, the "jump" action might be mapped to the spacebar by default.
- Input Rebinding: This allows players to *change* those mappings within the game. A player might want to change "jump" from the spacebar to the left shift key.

Why is this important?

- Player Preference: Different players find different control schemes more comfortable.
- Accessibility: Players with disabilities may need to use alternative control methods.

- Customization: It makes the game feel more personal and customizable.

A Conceptual Example in Rust:

```rust
Rust

use std::collections::HashMap;


struct InputMapping {

    mappings: HashMap<GameAction, InputEvent>,

}


impl InputMapping {

    fn new() -> Self {

        InputMapping {

            mappings: HashMap::new(),

        }

    }



    fn set_default_mappings(&mut self) {

        self.mappings.insert(GameAction::Jump,
InputEvent::Keyboard(KeyCode::Space));
```

```rust
        self.mappings.insert(GameAction::Fire,
InputEvent::Gamepad(GamepadButton::X));

        // ... default mappings

    }


    fn get_action_for_event(&self, event:
&InputEvent) -> Option<GameAction> {

        self.mappings.get(event).copied()

    }


    fn set_mapping(&mut self, action: GameAction,
event: InputEvent) {

        self.mappings.insert(action, event);

    }

}


fn main() {

    let mut input_mapping = InputMapping::new();

    input_mapping.set_default_mappings();


    // Simulate input events
```

```rust
    let event1 =
InputEvent::Keyboard(KeyCode::Space);

    let event2 =
InputEvent::Keyboard(KeyCode::LeftShift);



    // Get the action for an event

    if let Some(action) =
input_mapping.get_action_for_event(&event1) {

        println!("Action for spacebar: {:?}",
action);

    }



    // Rebind an action

    input_mapping.set_mapping(GameAction::Jump,
event2);



    // Get the action for the same event after
rebinding

    if let Some(action) =
input_mapping.get_action_for_event(&event1) {

        println!("Action for spacebar after
rebinding: {:?}", action);

    } else {

        println!("Spacebar is no longer Jump");
```

```
    }


    if let Some(action) =
input_mapping.get_action_for_event(&event2) {

        println!("Left Shift is now Jump: {:?}",
action);

    }

}
```

This shows how to store and change input preferences.

Handling Multiple Players: Coordinated Control

If your game allows more than one player (either on the same screen or online), you need a system to:

- Distinguish Input: You need to know which input came from which player.
- Assign Devices: You might let players choose their preferred controllers.
- Prevent Conflicts: If two players try to use the same key or button, you need a way to handle that.

Techniques:

- Player IDs: Give each player a unique ID, and tag input events with that ID.
- Device Selection: Let players choose their controllers in a menu.
- Input Contexts: Use input contexts to activate or deactivate certain input actions depending on the situation (e.g., in a menu, only menu navigation input is active).

Accessibility: Games for Everyone

Accessibility is about making your game playable by as many people as possible, including people with disabilities.

- Rebindable Controls: This is absolutely essential.
- Adjustable Sensitivity: Let players change mouse and controller sensitivity.
- Alternative Control Schemes: Offer simplified controls or different layouts.
- Assistive Technology Support: Try to make your game compatible with tools like screen readers or eye trackers.
- Clear Instructions: Provide easy-to-understand explanations of the controls.

Examples:

- An in-game option to toggle "sticky keys" (so players don't have to hold down Shift or Ctrl).
- A setting to adjust the "dead zone" on gamepad analog sticks (the area where input is ignored).
- A control scheme that uses fewer buttons for players who have limited mobility.

Exercise:

1. Explain in your own words why device abstraction is a good idea.
2. Describe a situation where input buffering would be crucial for a game.
3. What are the advantages and disadvantages of input polling compared to event-driven input?
4. Design a data structure (in Rust) to store player-specific input mappings (e.g., each player has their own keybindings).
5. List and explain five different ways to make a game more accessible to players with disabilities.

6. Find an example of a game that has particularly good input customization options and explain what makes them effective.

By carefully considering these aspects, you can build an input system that feels great, works reliably, and welcomes a wider audience to enjoy your game!

5.2 Designing Flexible Game Logic

Game logic is the set of rules and systems that make your game tick. It's what dictates how things behave, interact, and respond to the player. Think of it as the game's internal operating system.

When we aim for "flexible" game logic, we're essentially trying to create a system that's:

- Easy to change: You can tweak parameters or add new features without rewriting huge chunks of code.
- Easy to expand: You can add new content or systems without breaking existing ones.
- Easy to maintain: Your code is organized and understandable, making it easier to fix bugs and update.

Here's how we can achieve this:

Modularity: The Power of Separation

The most fundamental principle is to break down your game's logic into smaller, independent units called *modules*. Each module handles a specific aspect of the game.

It's like building with components. You have a component for the engine, another for the wheels, another for the steering, and you put them together to make a car.

Similarly, in game development, you can have modules for:

- Movement: This module handles how characters or objects move in the game. It takes care of things like acceleration, velocity, collision detection, and different movement types (walking, running, flying).
- Combat: This module manages all the combat-related mechanics. It deals with attacks, damage calculation, hit points, special abilities, and AI combat behavior.
- Inventory: This module handles how players acquire, manage, use, and store items. It controls things like item properties, weight, stacking, and inventory limits.
- AI: This module controls the behavior of non-player characters (NPCs). It defines how they make decisions, react to the player, and interact with the game world.
- Physics: This module simulates the physical laws of your game world, including gravity, collisions, forces, and momentum.

Why is modularity so beneficial?

- Organization: Your code becomes much more structured. Instead of one giant, tangled mess, you have clearly defined sections.
- Readability: Each module is smaller and focuses on a single purpose, making it easier to understand and work with.
- Maintainability: If you need to change how movement works, you only need to touch the movement module, not the combat or inventory modules.
- Reusability: You might be able to reuse a movement module in different games or different parts of the same game.
- Collaboration: If you're working in a team, different developers can work on different modules without stepping on each other's toes.

Conceptual Rust Example:

```rust
Rust

// In a real project, these would likely be in
separate files.


mod movement {

    pub struct MovementSystem {

        // Data needed for movement (e.g.,
gravity, max speed)

        gravity: f32,

        max_speed: f32,

    }


    impl MovementSystem {

        pub fn new() -> Self {

            MovementSystem {

                gravity: 9.8,

                max_speed: 10.0,

            }

        }
```

```rust
        pub fn update(&mut self, /* character
position, velocity, input */) {

            // Logic to update character position
and velocity

            // based on gravity, input, etc.

        }

    }

}


mod combat {

    pub struct CombatSystem {

        // Data needed for combat (e.g., weapon
damage, attack cooldowns)

        weapon_damage: i32,

        attack_cooldown: f32,

    }


    impl CombatSystem {

        pub fn new() -> Self {

            CombatSystem {

                weapon_damage: 10,

                attack_cooldown: 0.5,
```

```rust
            }

        }


        pub fn handle_attack(&mut self, /*
attacker, target */) {

            // Logic to handle an attack,
calculate damage, etc.

        }

    }

}


// ... other modules (inventory, ai, etc.)


struct Game {

    movement_system: movement::MovementSystem,

    combat_system: combat::CombatSystem,

    // ... other systems

}


impl Game {

    fn new() -> Self {
```

```rust
        Game {

            movement_system:
movement::MovementSystem::new(),

            combat_system:
combat::CombatSystem::new(),

            // ... initialize other systems

        }

    }



    fn update(&mut self, /* game time, player
input, etc. */) {

        self.movement_system.update(/* ... */);

        // ... update other systems

    }



    fn handle_input(&mut self, /* player input
*/) {

        if /* player pressed attack button */ {

            self.combat_system.handle_attack(/*
... */);

        }

        // ... handle other input

    }
```

```
}


fn main() {

    let mut game = Game::new();

    // ... game loop

}
```

This example shows how we can structure our game logic into separate modules for movement and combat.

Data-Driven Design: The Power of External Data

Instead of hardcoding game data directly into your code, Data-Driven Design (DDD) encourages you to store it in external files or databases. This data defines the rules and content of your game.

Examples of game data that can be externalized:

- Character Stats: Health, attack power, defense, speed, etc.
- Weapon Properties: Damage, range, fire rate, accuracy, etc.
- Level Layouts: Positions of objects, terrain information, enemy spawn points, etc.
- Dialogue: Text for conversations with NPCs, quest descriptions, etc.
- Game Rules: Parameters that control game mechanics, such as gravity, player speed, or damage multipliers.

Why is this a good idea?

- Flexibility: You can change game parameters or add new content without having to recompile your code. This is incredibly useful for tweaking gameplay balance or adding new items.

- Modding Support: It makes it much easier for players to modify your game. They can edit data files to create new content or change game mechanics.
- Collaboration: Designers and programmers can work more independently. Designers can tweak stats or create levels without needing to involve programmers in code changes.
- Maintainability: It's easier to manage and update data when it's separate from the code. You can use specialized tools to edit and validate the data.

Conceptual Rust Example (using JSON):

```rust
Rust

use serde::Deserialize;

use std::fs;


#[derive(Deserialize)]

struct WeaponData {

    name: String,

    damage: i32,

    range: f32,

}



fn load_weapon_data(file_path: &str) ->
Result<WeaponData, Box<dyn std::error::Error>> {
```

```rust
    let file_content =
fs::read_to_string(file_path)?;

    let weapon_data: WeaponData =
serde_json::from_str(&file_content)?;

    Ok(weapon_data)

}


fn main() -> Result<(), Box<dyn
std::error::Error>> {

    let weapon_data =
load_weapon_data("data/weapon.json")?;

    println!("Weapon Name: {}",
weapon_data.name);

    println!("Weapon Damage: {}",
weapon_data.damage);

    println!("Weapon Range: {}",
weapon_data.range);

    Ok(())

}


// Example data/weapon.json file:

// {

//    "name": "Steel Sword",
```

```
//    "damage": 15,

//    "range": 2.0

// }
```

This example shows how to load weapon data from a JSON file using the serde crate. To change the weapon's damage, you simply edit the weapon.json file.

Component-Based Design: Building Objects from Parts

Component-Based Design (CBD) is a powerful way to structure game objects. Instead of relying heavily on inheritance (where classes inherit properties from parent classes), you build objects by composing them from smaller, reusable components.

Components: These are data containers that hold specific attributes or behaviors. They're like Lego bricks that you can attach to an object.

Examples:

- PositionComponent: Stores the object's position in the game world (x, y, z coordinates).
- VelocityComponent: Stores the object's speed and direction.
- HealthComponent: Stores the object's current health.
- RenderableComponent: Stores information about how the object should be rendered (mesh, texture, etc.).

Entities: These are just unique IDs that represent the actual game objects. An entity is essentially a container for components.

Systems: These are modules that operate on entities that have specific components. For example, a MovementSystem would update the PositionComponent based on the VelocityComponent.

Why is this design so useful?

- Flexibility: You can easily create a wide variety of game objects by combining different components. A character might have a PositionComponent, VelocityComponent, HealthComponent, and InventoryComponent, while a static object might only have a PositionComponent and RenderableComponent.
- Reusability: Components can be reused across different types of objects. For example, the HealthComponent can be used for players, enemies, and even destructible objects.
- Decoupling: Components are independent of each other, making the code more modular and easier to maintain.
- Performance: ECS (Entity Component System), a specific implementation of CBD, can be optimized for data locality, leading to significant performance improvements.

Conceptual Rust Example (using a basic ECS approach):

```rust
Rust


use std::collections::HashMap;



type Entity = u32; // Simple Entity ID



// Components (data only)

struct PositionComponent {
```

```
    x: f32,

    y: f32,

}


struct VelocityComponent {

    dx: f32,

    dy: f32,

}


struct HealthComponent {

    health: i32,

}


// World (stores entities and components)

struct World {

    positions: HashMap<Entity,
PositionComponent>,

    velocities: HashMap<Entity,
VelocityComponent>,

    healths: HashMap<Entity, HealthComponent>,

    next_entity_id: Entity,
```

```rust
}


impl World {

    fn new() -> Self {

        World {

            positions: HashMap::new(),

            velocities: HashMap::new(),

            healths: HashMap::new(),

            next_entity_id: 0,

        }

    }


    fn create_entity(&mut self) -> Entity {

        self.next_entity_id += 1;

        self.next_entity_id

    }


    fn add_component<T: 'static>(&mut self,
entity: Entity, component: T) {

        // Simplified component addition
```

```rust
        // In a real ECS, you would use a more
robust approach

        // (e.g., using type IDs)

        if let Some(pos) =
component.downcast_ref::<PositionComponent>() {

            self.positions.insert(entity,
component.downcast::<PositionComponent>().unwrap(
));

        } else if let Some(vel) =
component.downcast_ref::<VelocityComponent>() {

            self.velocities.insert(entity,
component.downcast::<VelocityComponent>().unwrap(
));

        } else if let Some(health) =
component.downcast_ref::<HealthComponent>() {

            self.healths.insert(entity,
component.downcast::<HealthComponent>().unwrap())
;

        }

    }


    // Systems (logic that operates on
components)

    fn movement_system(&mut self) {

        for (entity, velocity) in
&self.velocities {
```

```rust
            if let Some(position) =
self.positions.get_mut(entity) {

                position.x += velocity.dx;

                position.y += velocity.dy;

            }

        }

    }


    fn damage_system(&mut self, entity: Entity,
damage: i32) {

        if let Some(health) =
self.healths.get_mut(&entity) {

            health.health -= damage;

            println!("Entity {} took {} damage.
Health: {}", entity, damage, health.health);

        }

    }

}


fn main() {

    let mut world = World::new();
```

```
    let player = world.create_entity();

    world.add_component(player, PositionComponent
{ x: 0.0, y: 0.0 });

    world.add_component(player, VelocityComponent
{ dx: 1.0, dy: 0.0 });

    world.add_component(player, HealthComponent {
health: 100 });


    let enemy = world.create_entity();

    world.add_component(enemy, PositionComponent
{ x: 10.0, y: 0.0 });

    world.add_component(enemy, HealthComponent {
health: 50 });


    world.movement_system(); // Update positions

    world.damage_system(player, 10); // Damage
the player

}
```

This example shows how entities are composed of components, and systems operate on those components.

Scripting: Adding Dynamic Behavior

Using a scripting language to define parts of your game logic can provide a lot of flexibility. Scripting allows you to change game behavior without recompiling the main game code.

Why is scripting useful?

- Rapid Prototyping: You can quickly experiment with new gameplay mechanics or AI behaviors without having to go through the lengthy process of recompiling your entire game.
- Modding Support: It makes it much easier for players to create their own content and modify the game. They can write scripts to add new quests, characters, or gameplay features.
- Dynamic Updates: In some cases, you might even be able to update certain aspects of your game's logic without requiring players to download a new version of the game.
- Complex Events: Scripting is very helpful for handling complex, branching events in your game, such as dialogue trees, quest sequences, or cutscenes.

Approaches to Scripting:

- Embed a Scripting Language: You can integrate a popular scripting language like Lua, Python, or JavaScript into your Rust game. This involves using a library that allows your Rust code to execute scripts and interact with the scripting engine.
- Use Rust as a Scripting Language: You can design your game in a way that allows you to load and execute Rust code dynamically. This is a more advanced technique but can offer better performance and tighter integration with your game's code.

Conceptual Example (Embedding Lua):

Rust

```
// Requires a Lua embedding library (e.g., rlua
or mlua)
```

```rust
// This is a simplified illustration

// fn main() -> rlua::Result<()> {

//      let lua = rlua::Lua::new();


//      lua.context(|ctx| {

//          // Load a Lua script

//          ctx.load(r#"

//              function damage_enemy(enemy_id, damage)

//                  -- Call a Rust function to apply damage

//                  rust_damage_enemy(enemy_id, damage)

//              end

//          "#).exec()?;


//          // Set up a Rust function that can be called from Lua

//          let rust_damage_enemy = ctx.create_function_mut(|_, (enemy_id, damage): (i32, i32)| {
```

```
//                // Rust code to apply damage to
the enemy

//                println!("Applying {} damage to
enemy {}", damage, enemy_id);

//                Ok(())

//            })?;

//            ctx.globals().set("rust_damage_enemy",
rust_damage_enemy)?;


//            // Call the Lua function

//            let damage_enemy_fn =
ctx.globals().get::<_,
rlua::Function>("damage_enemy")?;

//            damage_enemy_fn.call((1, 15))?;


//            Ok(())

//        })?;


//      Ok(())

// }
```

This example shows the basic idea of how you could call Rust functions from Lua scripts to control game logic.

Event Systems: Decoupled Communication

Event systems provide a way for different parts of your game logic to communicate with each other without having direct dependencies. This makes your code more flexible and easier to maintain.

Events: These are messages that are broadcast throughout the game. They represent something that has happened.

Examples:

- PlayerPickedUpItemEvent: Indicates that the player has picked up an item.
- EnemyDiedEvent: Indicates that an enemy has been defeated.
- GamePausedEvent: Indicates that the game has been paused.

Event Listeners: These are parts of the code that subscribe to specific events and react when those events occur.

Benefits of Event Systems:

- Decoupling: Modules don't need to know about each other. They only need to know how to send and receive events. This reduces dependencies and makes the code more modular.
- Flexibility: You can easily add or remove listeners without changing the code that sends the events. This makes it easier to add new functionality or change existing behavior.
- Extensibility: It's easy to add new event types and listeners to handle them, making your game more extensible.

Conceptual Rust Example:

```rust
Rust

use std::collections::HashMap;


// Define an event type

enum GameEvent {

    PlayerPickedUpItem { item_name: String },

    EnemyDied { enemy_id: u32 },

    // ... other events

}


// Simple event bus (in a real game, this would be more sophisticated)

struct EventBus {

    listeners: HashMap<String, Vec<Box<dyn Fn(&GameEvent)>>>,

}


impl EventBus {

    fn new() -> Self {

        EventBus {
```

```rust
            listeners: HashMap::new(),

        }

    }


    fn subscribe<F: Fn(&GameEvent) +
'static>(&mut self, event_type: String, listener:
F) {

        self.listeners

            .entry(event_type)

            .or_insert_with(Vec::new)

            .push(Box::new(listener));

    }


    fn publish(&self, event: &GameEvent) {

        let event_type = match event {

            GameEvent::PlayerPickedUpItem { .. }
=> "PlayerPickedUpItem".to_string(),

            GameEvent::EnemyDied { .. } =>
"EnemyDied".to_string(),

            _ => return, // Ignore unknown events

        };
```

```rust
        if let Some(listeners) =
self.listeners.get(&event_type) {

            for listener in listeners {

                listener(event);

            }

        }

    }

}


fn main() {

    let mut event_bus = EventBus::new();


    // Subscribe a UI system to the
PlayerPickedUpItem event

event_bus.subscribe("PlayerPickedUpItem".to_strin
g(), |event| {

        if let GameEvent::PlayerPickedUpItem {
item_name } = event {

            println!("UI: Displaying message:
Player picked up {}", item_name);

        }

    });
```

```rust
    // Subscribe an inventory system to the same
event

event_bus.subscribe("PlayerPickedUpItem".to_strin
g(), |event| {

        if let GameEvent::PlayerPickedUpItem {
item_name } = event {

            println!("Inventory: Adding {} to
inventory", item_name);

        }

    });


    // Simulate a player picking up an item

    let pick_up_event =
GameEvent::PlayerPickedUpItem {

        item_name: "Sword".to_string(),

    };

    event_bus.publish(&pick_up_event);

}
```

This example shows how different systems (UI and inventory) can react to the same event (player picking up an item) without knowing about each other.

Exercise:

- Explain in your own words why modularity is important in game logic design.
- Give three examples of game data that could be stored externally using Data-Driven Design.
- Describe the advantages and disadvantages of using Component-Based Design compared to traditional inheritance.
- Choose a game you know well and describe how scripting might be used to implement a specific feature (e.g., a complex quest, a character's AI).
- Design a simple event system for a game and show how it could be used to handle a specific interaction (e.g., a player opening a door).
- Research and describe a game engine that heavily utilizes one of the architectural patterns discussed (modularity, DDD, ECS).

5.3 State Machines and Game Flow Management

Game flow management is essentially the art of orchestrating the sequence of events in your game. It's about controlling how the game progresses, from the moment the player starts it up to the credits rolling (or the "Game Over" screen).

A key tool for this is the **state machine**.

What is a State Machine?

A state machine is a computational model that can exist in only one of a finite number of states at any given time.[1] Think of it as having different "modes" or "phases" that your game can be in.

The state machine can transition from one state to another based on specific *events* or conditions.[2] Each state defines what the game is doing and how it responds to input.

To understand it better, let's use an analogy.

Think of a simple vending machine:

- States:
    - Idle: The machine is waiting for you to insert money.
    - AcceptingCoins: The machine is accepting coins.
    - SelectingProduct: You can choose a product.
    - DispensingProduct: The machine is dispensing your selection.
- Events:
    - InsertCoin: A coin is inserted.
    - SelectProduct: A product is selected.
    - ProductDispensed: The product is dispensed.

The vending machine transitions between these states based on these events. For example, it goes from Idle to AcceptingCoins when you InsertCoin.

Games work in a similar way, although their state machines are often much more complex.

Common Game States

Here are some typical states you'll find in many games:

- MainMenu: This is the first state the player sees. It allows them to start a new game, load a saved game, access options, or quit.
- Playing: This is the core gameplay state, where the player is actively interacting with the game world.
- Paused: This state allows the player to temporarily stop the game, usually to take a break or adjust settings.[3]

- GameOver: This state is entered when the player has lost or failed to achieve the game's objective.
- Loading: This state is used while the game is loading assets or transitioning between levels.[4]

Why Use State Machines?

- Organization: State machines provide a clear and structured way to manage the flow of your game.[5] They prevent you from having spaghetti code with confusing and tangled logic.
- Clarity: They make it easier to understand how the game transitions from one phase to another.
- Maintainability: They make it easier to modify the game's flow, add new states, or change the conditions for transitions.
- Debugging: They can help you identify and fix bugs related to game flow.[6]

Conceptual Rust Example

Let's illustrate how a basic game state machine might be represented in Rust. This example uses an enum to define the states and a match statement to handle transitions.

Rust

```
// Define the different states of the game


enum GameState {


    MainMenu,


    Playing,
```

```
    Paused,

    GameOver,

    Loading,

}




// Define possible input events that trigger
state transitions

enum InputEvent {

    StartGame,

    PauseGame,

    ResumeGame,

    QuitGame,

    LoadLevel,
```

```rust
    GameOver,

}



struct Game {

    state: GameState,

}



impl Game {

    fn new() -> Self {

        Game {

            state: GameState::MainMenu, // Start
in the main menu

        }
```

```rust
    }


    fn handle_input(&mut self, event: InputEvent)
{

        match self.state {

            GameState::MainMenu => {

                if event == InputEvent::StartGame
{

                    self.state =
GameState::Loading;

                    // Start loading the game in
another thread

                    // ...

                }

                // ... handle other main menu
input
```

```
                    }

            GameState::Loading => {

                    // Wait for loading to complete

                    // ...

                    // When loading is finished:

                    self.state = GameState::Playing;

            }

            GameState::Playing => {

                    if event == InputEvent::PauseGame
{

                            self.state =
GameState::Paused;

                    } else if event ==
InputEvent::GameOver {
```

```rust
                    self.state =
GameState::GameOver;

                }

                // ... handle gameplay input

            }

        GameState::Paused => {

            if event ==
InputEvent::ResumeGame {

                    self.state =
GameState::Playing;

                } else if event ==
InputEvent::QuitGame {

                    self.state =
GameState::MainMenu;

                }

                // ... handle pause menu input
```

```
            }


        GameState::GameOver => {


            if event == InputEvent::StartGame
{


                self.state =
GameState::Loading;


                // Restart the game


                // ...


            } else if event ==
InputEvent::QuitGame {


                self.state =
GameState::MainMenu;


            }


            // ... handle game over menu
input


        }
```

```rust
        }

    }


    fn update(&mut self) {

        match self.state {

            GameState::Playing => {

                // Update game logic (e.g.,
character movement, AI)

                // ...

            }


            GameState::MainMenu => {

                // Update main menu animations or
logic

                // ...
```

```
        }


        GameState::Paused => {

            // Update pause menu logic

            // ...

        }


        GameState::GameOver => {

            // Update game over screen logic

            // ...

        }


        GameState::Loading => {

            // Update loading screen logic

            // ...

        }
```

```rust
        }

    }

}



fn main() {

    let mut game = Game::new();

    // Simulate some input events

    game.handle_input(InputEvent::StartGame);

    game.update(); // Game is now in Loading
state

    // ... simulate loading time

    game.handle_input(InputEvent::LoadLevel); //
Simulate loading finished

    game.update(); // Game is now in Playing
state
```

```
    game.handle_input(InputEvent::PauseGame);

    game.update(); // Game is now in Paused state

    game.handle_input(InputEvent::ResumeGame);

    game.update(); // Game is back in Playing
state

    game.handle_input(InputEvent::GameOver);

    game.update(); // Game is now in GameOver
state

    game.handle_input(InputEvent::QuitGame);

    game.update(); // Game is back in MainMenu
state


    // ... game loop

}
```

In this example:

- We define the game's states using the GameState enum.
- We define events that trigger state transitions using the InputEvent enum.
- The Game struct holds the current state.
- The handle_input method takes an InputEvent and uses a match statement to determine the next state.
- The update method performs state-specific logic.

This is a simplified illustration. In a real game, you might use a more sophisticated state machine library or design pattern.

Exercise

1. Explain in your own words what a state machine is and why it's useful in game development.
2. List and describe five common game states.
3. Draw a state diagram for a simple platformer game, including states like MainMenu, Playing, Paused, GameOver, and transitions between them.
4. Describe how a state machine could be used to manage the flow of a complex cutscene in a game.
5. Research and describe a state machine library or pattern that you could use in Rust.
6. Extend the Rust code example above to include a Loading state and simulate a basic loading process.

Chapter 6: Physics and Collision Detection

Okay, let's talk about making our game worlds feel dynamic and interactive! We're going to explore physics and collision detection, which are essential for creating believable movement, interactions, and overall realism. This chapter will cover how to bring physics into your Rust games, detect when objects bump into each other, and optimize these systems for performance.

6.1 Integrating Physics Engines in Rust

Okay, let's talk about bringing physics into your Rust game. This is a crucial step for making your game world feel interactive and believable. We'll focus on how to use existing physics engines, which is the most common and efficient approach for most game developers.

Physics engines are specialized libraries that handle the complex calculations involved in simulating physical phenomena like gravity, collisions, and forces. They do the heavy lifting so you can focus on the game's design and gameplay.

Why Use a Physics Engine?

While you could write your own physics simulations from scratch (especially for very basic effects), using a physics engine offers significant advantages:

- Realism: Physics engines can simulate interactions with a high degree of accuracy, making your game world feel more convincing. Think about how objects bounce, slide, and collide in the real world. A good physics engine tries to replicate that.
- Efficiency: Physics engines are highly optimized for these complex calculations. They use techniques like spatial

partitioning (dividing the world into sections) and vectorized operations (performing calculations on multiple values at once) to run efficiently.

- Features: They provide a wide range of pre-built features, saving you a lot of development time. These features often include:
  - Rigid body dynamics (how solid objects move)
  - Collision detection (figuring out when objects touch)
  - Joint constraints (simulating hinges, springs, etc.)
  - And more.
- Development Speed: It's much faster to integrate a physics engine than to write your own from scratch. This allows you to focus on other aspects of your game.

The Integration Process: A Step-by-Step Guide

Integrating a physics engine into your Rust game generally involves these key steps:

1. Choosing a Physics Engine:
2. Setting Up the Physics World:
3. Creating Rigid Bodies:
4. Defining Shapes (Colliders):
5. Adding Forces and Torques:
6. Handling Collisions:
7. Synchronizing Game Objects:

Let's explore each of these in detail:

Choosing a Physics Engine

The first and perhaps most important step is selecting the right physics engine for your project. There are several options available, each with its own strengths and weaknesses.

Here are a few prominent ones, with a focus on their use within the Rust ecosystem:

Rapier:

- This is a pure Rust physics engine designed for both 2D and 3D simulations.

Strengths:

- Excellent performance, often competing with or surpassing C++ engines in certain scenarios.
- Relatively easy to use and integrates well with Rust's ownership and borrowing system.
- Well-maintained and actively developed.

Considerations:

- A very good general-purpose choice for Rust game developers.

Bevy Physics:

- This is a physics plugin specifically designed for the Bevy game engine (which is also written in Rust).

Strengths:

- Tightly integrated with Bevy's Entity Component System (ECS) architecture, leading to efficient data access and management.
- Leverages Bevy's data-oriented design principles for performance.
- Offers a smooth and consistent workflow if you're already using Bevy.

Considerations:

- Primarily intended for use within the Bevy engine.

PhysX:

- This is a powerful C++ physics engine developed by Nvidia. It's widely used in the game industry, especially for large-scale, graphically intensive games.

Strengths:

- Highly advanced features, including cloth simulation, fluid dynamics, and fracture modeling.
- Robust and mature, with years of development and optimization.

Considerations:

- Integrating PhysX with Rust typically involves using C++ bindings, which can introduce complexity and potential safety issues.
- May have a steeper learning curve compared to Rapier or Bevy Physics.

Box2D:

- This is a 2D physics engine that's often used for 2D games, such as platformers.

Strengths:

- Efficient and stable for 2D simulations.
- Well-established and widely used in 2D game development.

Considerations:

- Specifically for 2D games.
- Integration with Rust requires using bindings.

The best choice of physics engine depends on several factors:

- Dimensionality: Is your game 2D or 3D?

- Performance requirements: How many objects will be interacting, and how complex are the physics calculations?
- Complexity of physics: Do you need advanced features like soft body dynamics or fluid simulation?
- Ease of integration: How straightforward is it to set up the engine with your Rust code?
- Existing engine: If you're already using a game engine, does it have a preferred physics solution?

Setting Up the Physics World

Once you've chosen a physics engine, you'll typically need to initialize a "physics world." This is the container for all the physics-related data and simulations.

The physics world often has configurable parameters that you can adjust:

- Gravity: The direction and strength of the gravitational force.
- Solver settings: Parameters that control the accuracy and stability of the physics simulation.
- Timestep: The duration of each physics simulation step.

Creating Rigid Bodies

Rigid bodies are the objects in your game that will be affected by physics. A rigid body is an idealized object that doesn't deform. Think of things like:

- Boxes
- Spheres
- Platforms
- Characters (often approximated as capsules)

You'll create a rigid body within the physics engine to represent each of these objects in your game.

Rigid bodies have properties that define their physical behavior:

- Position: The object's location in the game world.
- Rotation: The object's orientation.
- Mass: How resistant the object is to changes in motion (inertia).
- Velocity: The object's speed and direction of movement.

Body Type:

- Static: The object is fixed and doesn't move (e.g., a wall).
- Dynamic: The object can move in response to forces and collisions (e.g., a ball).
- Kinematic: The object can be moved by your code but is still affected by collisions (e.g., a moving platform).

Defining Shapes (Colliders)

To detect collisions between rigid bodies, you need to define their shapes. These shapes are often called "colliders." The physics engine uses these colliders to determine if and how objects are touching.

Common collider shapes include:

- Boxes: For rectangular objects.
- Spheres: For round objects.
- Capsules: For objects with rounded ends (often used for characters).
- Convex Hulls: For more complex, but still convex (no indentations), shapes.

- Triangle Meshes: For highly detailed, concave shapes (these are more computationally expensive).

Choosing appropriate collider shapes is a trade-off between accuracy and performance. Simple shapes are faster to process, but they might not accurately represent the object's true form.

Adding Forces and Torques

To make rigid bodies move and interact, you need to apply forces and torques to them.

Forces:

- These are what cause linear motion.

Examples:

- Gravity
- Player input
- Explosions
- Friction

Torques:

- These are rotational forces that cause rigid bodies to rotate.

Handling Collisions

The physics engine will automatically detect when rigid bodies collide with each other. However, you need to write code to *respond* to these collisions.

This might involve:

- Applying Damage: If a projectile hits an enemy.
- Playing Sounds: When objects impact.
- Changing Game State: Triggering events or advancing the game.
- Preventing Overlapping: Adjusting object positions to ensure they don't pass through each other.

Physics engines often provide mechanisms like "collision callbacks" or events that your code can listen to and react to.

Synchronizing Game Objects

In your game, you'll likely have your own way of representing game objects (e.g., entities in an ECS, or custom structs). You need to keep these game objects synchronized with the rigid bodies in the physics engine. This typically involves:

- Updating the position and rotation of your game objects based on the physics simulation.
- Potentially updating the physics engine when a game object's position or rotation is changed outside of the physics simulation (e.g., by player input).

Conceptual Rust Example (using Rapier)

Here's a simplified example of how you might integrate the Rapier physics engine into a Rust game. This code aims to illustrate the core concepts and isn't a complete, production-ready implementation.

Rust

```
use rapier3d::prelude::*; // Import Rapier's
types and functions
```

```rust
struct PhysicsWorld {

    // Rapier's data structures to store rigid
bodies, colliders, etc.

    rigid_body_set: RigidBodySet,

    collider_set: ColliderSet,

    gravity: Vector<Real>,

    physics_pipeline: PhysicsPipeline,

    island_manager: IslandManager,

    broad_phase: BroadPhase,

    narrow_phase: NarrowPhase,

    joint_set: JointSet,

    ccd_solver: CCDSolver,

}


impl PhysicsWorld {

    fn new() -> Self {

        let gravity = vector![0.0, -9.81, 0.0];
// Gravity pointing downwards

        let physics_pipeline =
PhysicsPipeline::new(); // The main physics
simulation pipeline
```

```rust
        let island_manager =
IslandManager::new(); // Manages sleeping/waking
of objects

        let broad_phase = BroadPhase::new(); //
Narrows down potential collisions

        let narrow_phase = NarrowPhase::new(); //
Detects exact contact points

        let joint_set = JointSet::new(); // For
constraints between objects (e.g., hinges)

        let ccd_solver = CCDSolver::new(); // For
continuous collision detection (preventing fast
objects from passing through walls)


        PhysicsWorld {

            rigid_body_set: RigidBodySet::new(),

            collider_set: ColliderSet::new(),

            gravity,

            physics_pipeline,

            island_manager,

            broad_phase,

            narrow_phase,

            joint_set,

            ccd_solver,
```

```rust
        }

    }



    fn create_rigid_body(&mut self, position:
Point<Real>) -> RigidBodyHandle {

        let rigid_body =
RigidBodyBuilder::new_dynamic() // Create a
dynamic rigid body (one that can move)

            .translation(position.coords) // Set
the initial position

            .build(); // Build the rigid body

        self.rigid_body_set.insert(rigid_body) //
Add the rigid body to the physics world

    }



    fn create_collider(&mut self,
rigid_body_handle: RigidBodyHandle, shape: Shape)
-> ColliderHandle {

        let collider =
ColliderBuilder::new(shape) // Create a collider
with the given shape

            .restitution(0.7) // Set the
restitution (bounciness) of the collider (0.0 =
no bounce, 1.0 = perfect bounce)

            .build();
```

```rust
        self.collider_set.insert_with_parent(collider,
        rigid_body_handle, &mut self.rigid_body_set) //
        Attach the collider to the rigid body

    }


    fn step(&mut self) {

        let integration_parameters =
        IntegrationParameters::default(); // Parameters
        that control the physics simulation (e.g.,
        timestep)

        let mut hook = (); // A way to add custom
        logic during the simulation (not used in this
        example)

        let mut event_handler = (); // A way to
        handle collision events (not used in this
        example)



        self.physics_pipeline.step( // Advance
        the physics simulation by one timestep

            &self.gravity,

            &integration_parameters,

            &mut self.island_manager,

            &mut self.broad_phase,

            &mut self.narrow_phase,
```

```rust
            &mut self.rigid_body_set,

            &mut self.collider_set,

            &mut self.joint_set,

            &mut self.ccd_solver,

            &hook,

            &event_handler,

        );

    }

}



fn main() {

    let mut physics_world = PhysicsWorld::new();



    // Create a rigid body (e.g., a ball)

    let rigid_body_handle =
physics_world.create_rigid_body(point![0.0, 10.0,
0.0]); // Create a ball at (0, 10, 0)



    // Create a collider (e.g., a sphere) and
attach it to the rigid body

    let shape = Shape::ball(0.5); // Create a
sphere shape with a radius of 0.5
```

```
physics_world.create_collider(rigid_body_handle,
shape);


    // Simulate the physics world

    for _ in 0..100 { // Simulate for 100 steps

        physics_world.step(); // Perform one
physics simulation step


        // Get the position of the rigid body and
update the game object
        if let Some(rigid_body) =
physics_world.rigid_body_set.get(rigid_body_handl
e) {

            let position =
rigid_body.translation(); // Get the current
position of the ball

            println!("Ball position: {:?}",
position); // Print the position to the console

        }

    }

}
```

This simplified example demonstrates the basic workflow of using Rapier. A real-world implementation would involve more complex setup, collision handling, and synchronization with your game's rendering and logic systems.

Exercise:

1. Choose a Rust physics engine (Rapier or Bevy Physics) and explain its key features and advantages for game development in your own words.
2. Describe the concept of a "rigid body" in physics simulations and provide examples of common rigid body types used in games.
3. Explain the purpose of "colliders" and list the most common collider shapes used in games, along with their typical use cases.
4. Write a simple Rust function that creates a rigid body with a box collider using the chosen physics engine's API (Rapier or Bevy Physics).
5. Research and explain how the chosen physics engine handles gravity and basic collision response (e.g., bouncing).
6. Extend the Rapier example above to create a simple scene with multiple interacting objects (e.g., a stack of blocks falling onto a platform).

6.2 Advanced Collision Detection Techniques

Collision detection is the process of determining when two or more objects in a game are touching or overlapping. It's a fundamental part of physics simulations, gameplay mechanics, and even things like player interaction with the environment.

It's important to understand that collision detection isn't just a single technique. It's often a combination of different approaches, each with its own trade-offs between accuracy and computational cost.

Here's a detailed look at some of the advanced techniques we use:

1. Broad Phase Collision Detection: The Initial Cull

Think of searching for something in a large warehouse. You wouldn't check every single box, right? You'd first look for labels or sections to narrow down your search. Broad phase collision detection does the same thing for objects in your game. It's a fast, initial check to quickly eliminate pairs of objects that are obviously too far apart to be colliding.

Sweep and Prune:

- This technique is very efficient when objects tend to move primarily along one or a few axes. Imagine a 2D platformer where characters mainly move left and right.

How it works:

- You sort the objects based on their bounding boxes' positions along each axis (X, Y, and Z in 3D). A bounding box is a simple rectangular box that tightly encloses an object.
- Then, you "sweep" along these sorted lists, checking for overlaps. Only objects whose bounding boxes overlap on *all* axes are considered potential collisions.

Why it's good:

- Fast for scenes with limited movement complexity.

Bounding Volume Hierarchies (BVH):

- This method organizes objects into a tree-like hierarchy of bounding volumes. A bounding volume is a simple shape (like a box or sphere) that completely encloses an object or a group of objects.

How it works:

- You start with a large bounding volume that encloses the entire scene.
- You recursively subdivide this volume into smaller volumes, grouping objects together.
- To check for collisions, you traverse the tree. If two large bounding volumes don't overlap, you can quickly discard all the objects within them. You only need to check for collisions between objects within overlapping volumes.

Why it's good:

- Effective for complex scenes with many objects of varying sizes.

Spatial Partitioning:

- This technique divides the game world into smaller regions or cells.

How it works:

- Common partitioning methods include:
  - Grid: Dividing the world into a regular grid of squares (2D) or cubes (3D).
  - Quadtree (2D) / Octree (3D): Recursively dividing space into quadrants or octants.
  - You only check for collisions between objects that reside in the same cell or neighboring cells.

Why it's good:

- Simple to implement and efficient for scenes with a relatively even distribution of objects.

2. Narrow Phase Collision Detection: The Precise Analysis

After the broad phase has identified potential collisions, we need to perform more detailed checks to determine the exact nature of the contact. This is where narrow phase collision detection comes in.

Narrow phase algorithms are more computationally intensive than broad phase, but they provide much more accurate results.

Here are some common narrow phase techniques:

Separating Axis Theorem (SAT):

- This is a powerful technique for detecting collisions between *convex* polygons (in 2D) or polyhedra (in 3D). A convex shape is one where any line segment connecting two points inside the shape lies entirely inside the shape (no dents or holes).

How it works:

- The core idea is to project the shapes onto a series of axes (lines in 2D, planes in 3D). These axes are typically the normals (perpendiculars) to the edges or faces of the shapes.
- If there's *any* axis where the projections of the shapes don't overlap, then the shapes are *not* colliding.
- If the projections overlap on all axes, then the shapes are colliding.

Why it's good:

- Relatively efficient for convex shapes.
- Can also be used to calculate the minimum translation vector (MTV), which is the smallest distance you need to move one shape to separate it from the other. This is very useful for collision response (preventing objects from overlapping).

GJK (Gilbert–Johnson–Keerthi) Algorithm:

- This is a more general and versatile algorithm for detecting collisions between convex shapes.

How it works:

- GJK works by finding the closest points between two shapes. It uses the *Minkowski difference* (a mathematical operation on shapes) and iteratively refines a *simplex* (a simple geometric shape like a triangle or tetrahedron) to find the closest point.

Why it's good:

- Can handle a wider variety of convex shapes than SAT.
- Also provides information for collision response, such as the closest points and penetration depth.

Raycasting:

- This technique involves casting a ray (a line segment) from a point in space and checking if it intersects with any objects.

How it works:

- You define the origin and direction of the ray.
- You then calculate whether the ray intersects with the surfaces of any objects in the scene.

Why it's good:

- Very useful for:
  - Player-object interaction (e.g., clicking on an object).
  - Line of sight checks (e.g., for AI).
  - Projectile trajectories (e.g., checking if a bullet hits a target).

3. Collision Response: Reacting to Impact

Once you've detected a collision, you need to determine what happens as a result. This is called collision response.

Here are two common approaches:

Impulse-Based Collision Response:

- This is the most common approach for simulating realistic physics.

How it works:

- You calculate the *impulse*, which is a change in momentum, that needs to be applied to the colliding objects to change their velocities.
- The impulse is calculated based on factors like:
    - The masses of the objects.
    - Their velocities before the collision.
    - The *coefficient of restitution* (a value that determines how "bouncy" the objects are).
- This approach is good for simulating realistic bouncing, rebounding, and changes in momentum.

Penalty-Based Collision Response:

- This is a simpler approach, but it can be less stable.

How it works:

- When objects overlap, you apply forces to them to push them apart. The force is proportional to the amount of overlap.

Why it's good:

- Easier to implement in some situations.

Why it's not always ideal:

- Can lead to "springy" or jittery behavior if not carefully tuned.

Example: A Simplified SAT Implementation (2D Rectangles)

To illustrate the Separating Axis Theorem, let's create a simplified example in Rust that checks for collisions between 2D rectangles.

Rust

```rust
use std::f32::consts::PI;

#[derive(Debug, Copy, Clone)]

struct Point {

    x: f32,

    y: f32,

}

#[derive(Debug, Copy, Clone)]

struct Rectangle {

    center: Point,

    half_width: f32,
```

```rust
    half_height: f32,

    rotation: f32, // In radians

}

    // Function to project a rectangle
onto an axis

    fn project_rectangle(rect: &Rectangle, axis:
    Point) -> (f32, f32) {

    // Calculate the vertices of the
    rectangle

    let vertices = [

        Point {

            x: rect.center.x -
rect.half_width,

            y: rect.center.y -
rect.half_height,

        },

        Point {

            x: rect.center.x +
rect.half_width,

            y: rect.center.y -
rect.half_height,
```

```rust
        },

        Point {

            x: rect.center.x +
rect.half_width,

            y: rect.center.y +
rect.half_height,

        },

        Point {

            x: rect.center.x -
rect.half_width,

            y: rect.center.y +
rect.half_height,

        },

    ];

    let mut min = f32::INFINITY;

    let mut max = f32::NEG_INFINITY;

    // Rotate the vertices

    let cos_theta = rect.rotation.cos();

    let sin_theta = rect.rotation.sin();
```

```rust
    for vertex in &vertices {

        let rotated_x = rect.center.x +
(vertex.x - rect.center.x) * cos_theta -
(vertex.y - rect.center.y) * sin_theta;

        let rotated_y = rect.center.y +
(vertex.x - rect.center.x) * sin_theta +
(vertex.y - rect.center.y) * cos_theta;

        let projection = rotated_x * axis.x
+ rotated_y * axis.y;

        min = min.min(projection);

        max = max.max(projection);

    }

    (min, max)

}

// Function to check if two rectangles
collide using SAT

fn rectangles_collide(rect1: &Rectangle,
rect2: &Rectangle) -> bool {

    // Axes to check: the normals
(perpendiculars) of the rectangle edges

    let axes = [
```

```rust
        Point { x: 1.0, y: 0.0 }, // X-axis

        Point { x: 0.0, y: 1.0 }, // Y-axis

        Point {

            x: -(rect1.rotation + PI /
    2.0).sin(),

            y: (rect1.rotation + PI /
    2.0).cos(),

        },

        Point {

            x: -(rect2.rotation + PI /
    2.0).sin(),

            y: (rect2.rotation + PI /
    2.0).cos(),

        },

    ];

    // Check for overlap on each axis

    for axis in axes {

        let (min1, max1) =
    project_rectangle(rect1, axis);
```

```rust
        let (min2, max2) =
project_rectangle(rect2, axis);

        // If there's no overlap on this
axis, the rectangles don't collide

        if max1 < min2 || max2 < min1 {

            return false;

        }

    }

    // Overlap on all axes, so the
rectangles collide

    true

}


fn main() {

    let rect1 = Rectangle {

        center: Point { x: 0.0, y: 0.0 },

        half_width: 1.0,

        half_height: 1.0,
```

```rust
        rotation: 0.0,

    };

    let rect2 = Rectangle {

        center: Point { x: 1.5, y: 0.5 },

        half_width: 1.0,

        half_height: 1.0,

        rotation: PI / 4.0, // 45 degrees

    };


    if rectangles_collide(&rect1, &rect2) {

        println!("Rectangles collide!");

    } else {

        println!("Rectangles do not
collide.");

    }

}
```

Key points in this example:

- We define Point and Rectangle structs to represent the shapes.
- project_rectangle calculates the projection of a rectangle onto a given axis, including rotation.
- rectangles_collide implements the SAT to check for overlap on the relevant axes.

Exercise:

1. Explain the purpose of broad phase and narrow phase collision detection, and provide a real-world analogy for each.
2. Describe the Separating Axis Theorem (SAT) in detail, including its strengths and limitations.
3. Explain how raycasting works and list three distinct uses for it in game development.
4. Compare and contrast impulse-based and penalty-based collision response, discussing their advantages and disadvantages.
5. Extend the SAT example above to handle collisions between rectangles that can be rotated.
6. Research and describe how collision detection is used in a specific game genre that you are interested in (e.g., fighting games, racing games, platformers).

6.3 Optimizing Physics Simulations

Okay, let's talk about making sure our physics simulations run smoothly and efficiently. This is a really crucial aspect of game development, because simulating physics can be very demanding on the computer, especially when you have a lot of objects moving around and interacting. We need to find ways to make things run fast without sacrificing too much of that believable physics.

Here's a detailed exploration of the most common and effective optimization strategies:

1. Sleeping: The Efficiency of Stillness

Think about a game scene with a bunch of objects. Some might be actively moving and colliding, but many others are likely to be stationary – a box sitting on the floor, a rock that's been still for a long time. It's inefficient to keep performing physics calculations for these motionless objects as if they were in constant motion.

How it works:

- The physics engine continuously monitors the rigid bodies (the objects affected by physics).
- If a body remains at rest (or has a very low velocity) for a certain duration, the engine puts it into a "sleeping" state.
- While a body is sleeping, the physics calculations for it are essentially paused. The engine doesn't update its position, velocity, or check for collisions. This saves processing power.
- If a sleeping body is affected by a significant force, a collision, or any other event that causes it to move, it "wakes up," and the simulation resumes.

Why it's good:

- Drastically reduces the computational load, especially in scenes with many static or resting objects.
- Improves overall performance, allowing for more complex simulations or higher frame rates.

Real-world example:

- In a game with a large number of debris pieces after an explosion, most of those pieces will eventually come to rest. The physics engine can put them to sleep, freeing up resources to simulate other, more active parts of the scene.

2. Substepping: Achieving Finer-Grained Accuracy

Think about filming a very fast-moving object with a camera. If you only take a few pictures per second, the object might appear blurry, or its motion might seem jerky. But if you take many pictures per second, the motion will be much smoother and more accurate.

Substepping in physics is similar. It's like taking more "snapshots" of the physics simulation within a single frame of your game.

How it works:

- Instead of updating the physics simulation once per game frame, you divide the frame into smaller time intervals called "substeps."
- The physics engine performs its calculations (applying forces, detecting collisions, updating positions, etc.) multiple times per frame, once for each substep.

Why it's good:

- Increases the accuracy and stability of the simulation, particularly for:
  - Fast-moving objects: Reduces the likelihood of objects "tunneling" (passing through other objects

because the simulation didn't detect the collision due to large movements between frames).

- ○ Simulations with strong forces or rapid changes in velocity.
- Results in smoother and more realistic motion.

Trade-off:

- Substepping increases the computational cost because the physics engine has to do more work per frame.
- You need to carefully choose the number of substeps to find a balance between accuracy and performance.

Real-world example:

- In a racing game, substepping can improve the accuracy of collision detection between cars traveling at high speeds, preventing them from clipping through each other.

3. Multithreading: Unleashing Parallel Power

Modern CPUs have multiple cores, which can perform different tasks simultaneously. Physics simulations can often be parallelized to take advantage of this.

How it works:

- The physics engine divides the simulation into smaller, independent tasks.
- These tasks are then distributed across the available CPU cores, allowing them to be executed concurrently.

- For example, calculating collisions between different groups of objects can be done on separate cores.

Why it's good:

- Provides a significant performance boost, especially on systems with many cores.
- Enables more complex and detailed physics simulations.

Challenges:

- Requires careful management of threads and synchronization to avoid issues like:
  - Race conditions (where threads access shared data in an unpredictable and incorrect order).
  - Data corruption.
  - Deadlocks (where threads get stuck waiting for each other).

Real-world example:

- A game with a large number of particles (e.g., for explosions or smoke effects) can use multithreading to calculate the movement and interactions of those particles in parallel.

4. Approximations: The Art of Simplification

In some cases, you might not need perfect accuracy in your physics simulation. You can use approximations to reduce the computational cost.

How it works:

- Use simpler shapes for collision detection. For example, approximate a complex object with a bounding box or a sphere.
- Simplify physics calculations. For example, use a less detailed friction model or ignore certain forces.

Why it's good:

- Reduces the amount of work the CPU has to do.
- Can be a good trade-off when visual fidelity is more important than perfect physical realism.

Real-world example:

- In a large-scale battle scene in a strategy game, you might use simplified physics for distant units, focusing on more detailed simulation for units closer to the player's view.

5. Spatial Partitioning: Dividing the Space

We discussed spatial partitioning in the context of collision detection, but it's also a valuable optimization technique for physics simulations in general.

How it works:

- Divide the game world into smaller regions or cells.
- Only consider interactions between objects that are in the same or neighboring cells.

Why it's good:

- Reduces the number of collision checks and other physics calculations that need to be performed.
- Improves performance in large, complex scenes with many objects.

Real-world example:

- An open-world game might use spatial partitioning to only simulate the physics of objects in the player's immediate vicinity, ignoring objects in distant areas.

Example: A Simplified Substepping Illustration

Let's create a very basic example to illustrate the concept of substepping in Rust. This is a simplified representation and not a full physics engine.

```rust
Rust

struct Object {

    position: f32,

    velocity: f32,

}



fn simulate_object(object: &mut Object, timestep:
f32, gravity: f32) {
```

```rust
    // Simulate the effect of gravity

    object.velocity += gravity * timestep;

    // Simulate movement based on velocity

    object.position += object.velocity *
timestep;

}


fn main() {

    let mut object = Object {

        position: 0.0,

        velocity: 0.0,

    };



    let total_time = 1.0; // Total simulation
time (e.g., 1 second)

    let frame_rate = 60.0; // Target frame rate
(e.g., 60 frames per second)

    let num_frames = (total_time * frame_rate) as
usize; // Number of frames
```

```rust
// Version 1: No Substepping

let timestep = total_time / num_frames as
f32; // Time per frame

println!("No Substepping:");

let mut simple_object = Object {

    position: 0.0,

    velocity: 0.0,

};

for _ in 0..num_frames {

    simulate_object(&mut simple_object,
timestep, 1.0); // Simulate with gravity = 1.0

    println!("Position: {}",
simple_object.position);

}



// Version 2: With Substepping (e.g., 4
substeps per frame)

let substeps = 4; // Number of substeps per
frame
```

```rust
    let substep_timestep = timestep / substeps as
f32; // Time per substep

    println!("\nWith Substepping:");

    let mut substep_object = Object {

        position: 0.0,

        velocity: 0.0,

    };

    for _ in 0..num_frames {

        for _ in 0..substeps {

            simulate_object(&mut substep_object,
substep_timestep, 1.0);

        }

        println!("Position: {}",
substep_object.position);

    }

}
```

In this example:

- We have a simple Object with position and velocity.
- simulate_object updates the object's state based on gravity and velocity.

- The main function simulates the object's motion over a period of time.
- The "No Substepping" version updates the object's state once per frame.
- The "With Substepping" version updates the object's state multiple times per frame (4 times in this example), leading to a more accurate simulation, especially if the force of gravity is changing rapidly or if there are collisions.

Exercise:

1. Explain in your own words why optimizing physics simulations is crucial for achieving good game performance and providing a smooth player experience.
2. Describe how sleeping can be used to reduce the computational cost of physics simulations, and provide a real-world example from a game where this technique would be particularly effective.
3. Compare and contrast the advantages and disadvantages of using substepping in physics simulations, considering both the accuracy of the simulation and the performance impact.
4. Research and explain how a specific physics engine (e.g., Rapier, Bevy Physics) implements multithreading to speed up simulations, focusing on the techniques it uses to manage threads and avoid common problems like race conditions.
5. Provide examples of how approximations can be used to optimize physics simulations in different game genres (e.g., racing games, fighting games, strategy games), explaining the trade-offs involved in each case and the impact on the player experience.
6. Extend the simplified substepping example above to simulate a simple collision with a stationary ground plane and compare the results of the object's motion and the collision response (e.g., how the object bounces) with and

without substepping. Analyze how the accuracy of the collision simulation is affected by the number of substeps.

Chapter 7: Audio and Sound Effects

Okay, let's talk about making our games sound as good as they look! We're going to explore audio and sound effects, which are essential for creating immersive and engaging experiences. This chapter covers integrating audio libraries, implementing spatial audio, and optimizing audio playback.

7.1 Integrating Audio Libraries

Okay, let's talk about how we bring sound into our games. We rarely handle audio from scratch; instead, we rely on audio libraries. These are software tools that make working with sound much easier.

Think of audio libraries as specialized toolkits. They provide the functions and capabilities we need to play, manipulate, and manage sound in our games, without us having to deal with the low-level complexities of audio processing.

Why Use Audio Libraries?

Consider all the tasks involved in playing even a simple sound:

- Decoding Audio Files: Audio files come in various formats (MP3, WAV, Ogg Vorbis, etc.). Each format uses a different way of encoding the sound data. Audio libraries handle the decoding process, converting the encoded data into raw audio that the computer can play.
- Controlling Playback: You need to be able to start, stop, pause, resume, loop, and adjust the volume of sounds. Audio libraries provide functions for these playback controls.
- Mixing Audio: In most games, multiple sounds play simultaneously (music, sound effects, character voices).

Audio libraries handle the mixing process, combining the audio signals from different sources to create a coherent and balanced sound output.

- Outputting Audio: Finally, the audio data needs to be sent to the computer's audio output device (speakers, headphones). Audio libraries manage this communication with the sound hardware.

Trying to handle all these tasks manually would be extremely complex and time-consuming. Audio libraries abstract away the low-level details, allowing us to focus on the creative aspects of sound design.

The Integration Process: A Step-by-Step Overview

Integrating an audio library into your Rust game generally involves these key steps:

1. Choosing an Audio Library: Selecting the right library for your project.
2. Loading Audio Files: Reading sound data from files.
3. Playing Sounds: Controlling the playback of loaded audio.
4. Mixing Sounds: Combining multiple audio sources.
5. Applying Audio Effects: Enhancing sounds with processing techniques.

Let's examine each of these steps in detail:

1. Choosing an Audio Library

The first step is to select an audio library that meets the specific requirements of your game. Several options are available, each with its own strengths and weaknesses.

Here are some of the most relevant choices for Rust developers:

Symphonia:

- A pure Rust audio decoding and demuxing library.

What it does: Symphonia's primary purpose is to read and decode audio from various file formats. It's designed to be flexible and efficient at this specific task. It doesn't handle audio playback directly.

Why it's useful: If you need fine-grained control over audio decoding or if you need to support a wide range of audio formats, Symphonia is a good choice. You might use Symphonia to decode an MP3 file and then pass the decoded audio data to another library (like Rodio) for playback.

Example: Imagine you're building a game that allows players to load their own music files. Symphonia could be used to decode those files, regardless of their format.

Rodio:

- A Rust audio playback library built on top of Symphonia.

What it does: Rodio provides a simple and easy-to-use API for playing audio. It handles decoding (using Symphonia), mixing, and outputting audio to your computer's speakers or headphones.

Why it's useful: Rodio is a great choice for many game projects where you need straightforward audio playback without requiring very low-level control. It's suitable for playing sound effects, background music, and other common game audio elements.

Example: You could use Rodio to play the sound of a sword clashing, the background music for a level, or the voice lines of characters.

CPAL:

- A cross-platform audio input/output library for Rust.

What it does: CPAL gives you more direct control over audio streams, allowing you to work with audio devices (speakers, microphones) at a lower level. It's designed for applications that need more advanced audio processing.

Why it's useful: If you're developing a game that needs to work with real-time audio input (like voice chat) or needs to perform complex audio manipulation, CPAL might be necessary.

Example: CPAL could be used to implement a system where the player's voice is processed and distorted before being transmitted to other players in a multiplayer game.

FMOD:

- A commercial audio engine that provides a comprehensive set of audio features.

What it does: FMOD handles everything from basic playback to complex 3D audio, effects processing, and mixing. It's often used in larger game productions with high audio quality requirements.

Why it's useful: If you need professional-grade audio capabilities and are willing to pay for a license, FMOD is a powerful option.

Considerations: FMOD is not a Rust library; you'd need to use foreign function interface (FFI) bindings to access it from your Rust code, which can add complexity.

Key Factors for Choosing an Audio Library:
- Ease of Use: How easy is it to learn and use the library's API?
- Features: Does the library provide the features you need (e.g., 3D audio, effects processing, real-time mixing)?
- Performance: Is the library efficient enough for your game's performance requirements?
- Platform Support: Does the library work on all the platforms you're targeting (e.g., Windows, macOS, Linux, web)?
- Licensing: Are there any licensing fees or restrictions associated with the library?

2. Loading Audio Files

Once you've selected an audio library, you'll need to load your sound files into your game. This process varies depending on the library and the specific audio file format.

Common Audio File Formats:

- WAV: Uncompressed audio (high quality, large file size).
- MP3: Compressed audio (smaller file size, some quality loss).
- Ogg Vorbis: Another compressed audio format (good balance of quality and size).

Loading Methods:

- In-Memory Loading: The entire audio file is read into memory before playback. This is suitable for smaller sound effects.
- Streaming: The audio data is read from the file in chunks during playback. This is more memory-efficient for larger files like background music.

3. Playing Sounds

Audio libraries provide functions to control the playback of loaded audio. Common playback controls include:

- Start/Stop: Begin and end playback.
- Pause/Resume: Temporarily halt and restart playback.
- Volume Control: Adjust the loudness of the sound.
- Playback Speed: Control the speed at which the sound plays.
- Looping: Play the sound repeatedly.

- Panning: Control the balance between the left and right speakers.

4. Mixing Sounds

In most games, multiple sounds play simultaneously. This requires mixing, which is the process of combining the audio signals from different sources into a single output signal.

- Why mixing is necessary: If you simply add the raw audio signals together, they can "clip" (exceed the maximum amplitude), resulting in distortion.
- How audio libraries handle mixing: They often provide functions to perform mixing, ensuring that the output signal stays within acceptable levels.

5. Applying Audio Effects

Many audio libraries allow you to apply various effects to sounds to enhance them or create specific atmospheres. Common audio effects include:

- Reverb: Simulates the echoes and reflections of sound in a space, making sounds feel like they're in a room, hall, etc.
- Echo: Creates distinct repetitions of a sound.
- Distortion: Alters the sound to make it rough or gritty.
- Equalization (EQ): Adjusts the balance of different frequencies in a sound, allowing you to make it sound brighter, warmer, etc.

Example: Basic Audio Playback with Rodio

Here's a simple example of how to play a sound file using the Rodio library in Rust:

Rust

```rust
use rodio::{Sink, Source, OutputStream};

use std::fs::File;

use std::io::BufReader;

fn main() -> Result<(), Box<dyn
std::error::Error>> {

    // Get a handle to the default audio
output device

    let (_stream, handle) =
OutputStream::try_default()?;

    let sink = Sink::try_new(&handle)?;

    // Load a sound file

    let file = File::open("my_sound.wav")?;

    let buffered_reader =
BufReader::new(file);

    // Decode the sound file

    let source =
rodio::Decoder::new(buffered_reader)?;

    // Add the sound to the sink to play it

    sink.append(source);
```

```
    // The sound plays in the background, so
we need to keep the program running

    std::thread::sleep(std::time::Duration::from
_secs(5000)); // Sleep for 5 seconds



    Ok(())


}
```

This example shows the basic steps of playing a sound file with Rodio.

Exercise:

1. Choose a Rust audio library (Rodio or CPAL) and explain its key features and advantages for game development, providing specific examples of the types of games or audio tasks it would be suitable for.
2. Describe the process of loading an audio file into your game, explaining the trade-offs between different audio file formats (WAV, MP3, Ogg Vorbis) in terms of quality, file size, and decoding speed.
3. Write a simple Rust function that uses your chosen audio library to play a sound file and control its volume, including error handling for file loading and playback issues.
4. Explain the concept of audio mixing and why it's important when playing multiple sounds simultaneously in a game, providing a real-world analogy to illustrate the problem of clipping.
5. Research and describe three common audio effects (reverb, echo, distortion) and explain how they can be used creatively to enhance the audio experience in a game,

providing examples of specific game genres where each effect is often used.

6. Extend the Rodio example above to play two sound files simultaneously and control the volume and panning of each sound, demonstrating basic audio mixing and spatialization.

7.2 Spatial Audio Implementation

Okay, let's talk about how we make sounds in our games feel like they're coming from specific places. This is called spatial audio, or sometimes 3D audio, and it's a huge part of creating immersive and believable game environments.

Spatial audio goes beyond just playing a sound. It's about simulating how sound behaves in the real world, so players can pinpoint where sounds are coming from and get a better sense of their surroundings.

Here's a breakdown of the key concepts and techniques involved:

1. Sound Sources: Where the Sound Begins

The first thing we need to understand is the idea of a *sound source*. This is the virtual location in your game world where a sound originates. It's the point from which the sound waves are considered to be emanating.

Examples of Sound Sources:

- An enemy's footsteps
- The explosion of a grenade
- The sound of a character's voice
- The ambient sounds of a forest (birds, wind, etc.)

Each sound source has properties that define its behavior:

- Position: The 3D coordinates of the source in the game world.
- Velocity: How the source is moving (this is important for the Doppler effect).
- Direction (sometimes): The direction in which the sound is strongest (e.g., for a megaphone).

2. Listener: The Player's Ears

Next, we need the *listener*. This represents the player's "ears" in the game world. It's usually the position and orientation of the player's camera.

Listener Properties:

- Position: The 3D coordinates of the listener.
- Orientation: The direction the listener is facing.

3. Distance Attenuation: Sound Fades Away

One of the most fundamental aspects of how sound works is that it gets quieter as you move further away from the source. This is called distance attenuation.

How it works:

- Audio libraries provide attenuation models or functions that calculate the volume of a sound based on the distance between the sound source and the listener.
- These models often use mathematical formulas to simulate the inverse square law (sound intensity decreases with the square of the distance).

- Game developers often tweak the attenuation parameters to achieve the desired effect.

Why it's important:

- Distance attenuation is crucial for creating a sense of scale and depth in the game world.
- It helps players understand how far away objects are and where sounds are coming from.

Example:

- The sound of a distant explosion should be much quieter than the sound of an explosion nearby.

4. Panning: Left and Right Balance

Our ears use the difference in arrival time and intensity of sound at each ear to determine the horizontal direction of a sound source. This is called panning.

How it works:

- Audio libraries simulate panning by adjusting the volume of the sound in the left and right speakers (or headphones) based on the sound source's horizontal position relative to the listener.
- If a sound source is directly in front of the listener, the sound is played equally in both speakers.
- If the source is to the left, the sound is louder in the left speaker and quieter in the right speaker.

Why it's important:

- Panning helps players distinguish between sounds coming from the left and right sides of the game world.
- It adds a sense of directionality and spatial awareness.

Example:

- If an enemy is walking to the player's left, the sound of their footsteps should be louder in the left speaker.

5. Doppler Effect: The Pitch Shift of Motion

You've probably noticed that the pitch of a siren changes as it approaches and recedes from you. This is the Doppler effect.

How it works:

- Audio libraries simulate the Doppler effect by adjusting the playback speed (and therefore the pitch) of a sound based on the relative velocity between the sound source and the listener.
- When the source is approaching, the sound waves are compressed, resulting in a higher pitch.
- When the source is receding, the sound waves are stretched, resulting in a lower pitch.

Why it's important:

- The Doppler effect adds realism to the movement of objects in the game world.

- It can also provide cues about the speed and direction of moving objects.

Example:

- The sound of a speeding car engine should change pitch as the car passes the player.

6. Occlusion and Obstruction: Sound Through Barriers

In the real world, sound waves are affected by obstacles. They can be blocked (occluded) or muffled (obstructed) by walls, doors, and other objects.

How it works:

- Some advanced audio engines simulate occlusion and obstruction by:
    - Checking if there's a direct line of sight between the sound source and the listener.
    - Calculating how much of the sound is blocked by obstacles.
    - Applying filters to the sound to simulate muffling.

Why it's important:

- Occlusion and obstruction make the game world feel more believable and dynamic.
- They can also be used for gameplay purposes, such as allowing players to use sound to locate enemies behind walls.

Example:

- The sound of a character's voice should be muffled if they're behind a closed door.

Simplified Example (Conceptual Rust)

It's tricky to provide a fully working spatial audio example in a short snippet because it relies heavily on the specific capabilities of the audio library you're using. However, here's a simplified conceptual example in Rust to illustrate the core principles:

Rust

```rust
struct SoundSource {

    position: [f32; 3],

    sound_buffer: /* ... */, // Some
representation of the sound data

}


struct Listener {

    position: [f32; 3],
```

```rust
    orientation: /* ... */, //
Representing the direction the listener
is facing



}


fn apply_distance_attenuation(source:
&SoundSource, listener: &Listener,
volume: f32) -> f32 {


    let dx = listener.position[0] -
source.position[0];


    let dy = listener.position[1] -
source.position[1];


    let dz = listener.position[2] -
source.position[2];


    let distance = (dx * dx + dy * dy +
dz * dz).sqrt();


    // Simple attenuation model (you'd
likely use a more sophisticated one)


    let attenuated_volume = volume /
(1.0 + distance);
```

```rust
        attenuated_volume.clamp(0.0, 1.0)
// Ensure volume is between 0 and 1


}


// (Panning and Doppler effect would be
more complex and depend on the audio
library)


fn main() {

    let source = SoundSource {

        position: [5.0, 0.0, 0.0],

        sound_buffer: /* ... */,

    };

    let listener = Listener {

        position: [0.0, 0.0, 0.0],

        orientation: /* ... */,

    };
```

```rust
    let original_volume = 0.8;


    let attenuated_volume =
apply_distance_attenuation(&source, &listener,
original_volume);


        println!("Original volume: {}",
    original_volume);


        println!("Attenuated volume: {}",
    attenuated_volume);


        // (You would then use an audio
    library to play the sound with the
    attenuated volume)


    }
```

This example shows a simplified distance attenuation calculation. Real-world spatial audio implementations involve more complex math and rely on the features provided by audio libraries.

Exercise

1. Explain in your own words the importance of spatial audio for creating immersive game experiences.
2. Describe the role of a "sound source" and a "listener" in a spatial audio system.

3. Explain how distance attenuation affects the perceived volume of a sound and why this is important.
4. Describe the Doppler effect and give a real-world example of how it changes the sound we hear.
5. Research and describe how a specific audio engine or library (e.g., FMOD, Wwise, or a feature of a game engine) implements occlusion and obstruction.
6. Design a simple scenario in a game (e.g., a player walking through a forest) and describe how you would use spatial audio to enhance the player's experience.

7.3 Optimizing Audio Playback

Okay, let's talk about making sure the audio in our games performs well. While it might not seem as demanding as graphics, audio playback and processing can still have an impact on performance, especially when dealing with many sounds or complex audio effects. We want our audio to enhance the game, not hinder it.

Here's a breakdown of the key optimization techniques for audio playback:

1. Audio File Formats: Choosing the Right Container

The format you choose to store your audio files can significantly affect both file size and playback efficiency.

Uncompressed Formats:

Examples: WAV, PCM

Characteristics: Store audio data without any compression. This means the audio quality is the highest possible, but the file sizes can be very large.

Performance: Uncompressed audio is generally the fastest to play back because the computer doesn't need to do any decoding.

Use Cases: Short, critical sound effects where latency (delay) is crucial and file size is less of a concern.

Compressed Formats:

Examples: Ogg Vorbis, MP3, AAC

Characteristics: Store audio data in a compressed form, reducing file size. This means some audio data is discarded, leading to a slight loss in quality.

Performance: Compressed audio requires decoding before playback, which takes CPU time. The amount of CPU time depends on the complexity of the compression algorithm.

Use Cases: Background music, longer sound effects, and audio where file size is a major concern (e.g., streaming audio).

Trade-offs:

Quality vs. File Size: Uncompressed formats offer the best quality but at the cost of larger files. Compressed formats offer smaller file sizes but with some quality reduction.

CPU Usage vs. Storage/Bandwidth: Compressed audio requires CPU time for decoding, while uncompressed audio consumes more storage space or bandwidth.

Real-world example:

- A short sound effect like a gunshot might be stored as a WAV file for its fast playback and high quality.
- Background music might be stored as an Ogg Vorbis file to save disk space without significantly impacting the player's perception of quality.

2. Sound Caching: Keeping It Handy

Loading audio files from the disk every time they need to be played can be slow, especially if you have many frequently used sounds. Sound caching helps to mitigate this.

How it works:

- Frequently used sound data is loaded into memory (RAM) when the game starts or when needed.
- When the game needs to play a sound, it can retrieve it directly from memory, which is much faster than reading from the disk.

Why it's good:

- Reduces latency (delay) in sound playback, making the game feel more responsive.
- Improves overall performance by minimizing disk access.

Real-world example:

- The sound of a player's footsteps or weapon firing is likely to be cached because these sounds occur frequently.

3. Voice Limiting: Preventing Overload

The audio system of a computer has a limited capacity to play sounds simultaneously. If you try to play too many sounds at once, it can lead to performance problems or even audio glitches. Voice limiting helps to prevent this.

How it works:

- The audio system keeps track of the number of "voices" (individual sounds) that are currently playing.
- When a new sound needs to be played, the system checks if the maximum number of voices has been reached.
- If it has, the system might:
    - Stop the oldest or least important sound.
    - Refuse to play the new sound.
    - Prioritize sounds based on their importance (e.g., player actions are more important than background ambience).

Why it's good:

- Prevents audio overload and ensures smooth audio playback.
- Maintains performance, especially in scenes with many sound effects.

Real-world example:

- In a complex battle scene, the game might limit the number of simultaneous explosions and weapon fire sounds to avoid audio stuttering.

4. Streaming: Handling the Long Haul

For long audio files, like background music or lengthy dialogue, loading the entire file into memory at once can be inefficient. Streaming provides a better approach.

How it works:

- The audio data is read from the disk in small chunks and played back as it's being read.
- Only a small portion of the audio file is in memory at any given time.

Why it's good:

- Saves memory, allowing you to use it for other game resources.
- Enables playback of very long audio files without requiring excessive RAM.

Real-world example:

- Background music in a level is almost always streamed to avoid loading the entire track into memory.

5. Audio Compression: Reducing the Data Load

If you're processing audio in real-time (e.g., for voice chat or audio effects), you might need to compress the audio data to reduce the amount of data that needs to be transmitted or processed.

How it works:

- Audio compression algorithms remove redundant or less perceptually important parts of the audio data.
- This reduces the data size but also introduces some loss in audio quality.

Why it's good:

- Reduces bandwidth usage for network transmission (e.g., in online games).
- Reduces processing overhead for real-time audio effects.

Real-world example:

- Voice chat applications use audio compression to reduce the amount of data that needs to be sent over the internet, improving latency and bandwidth usage.

Example: Streaming Audio (Conceptual)

It's challenging to provide a complete, working streaming example without relying on a specific audio library's implementation. However, here's a conceptual illustration of how streaming might work in Rust:

```
Rust
```

```rust
use std::fs::File;

use std::io::{BufReader, Read};


fn stream_audio(file_path: &str, chunk_size:
usize) -> Result<(), Box<dyn std::error::Error>>
{

    let file = File::open(file_path)?;

    let mut reader = BufReader::new(file);

    let mut buffer = vec![0; chunk_size];


    loop {

        let bytes_read = reader.read(&mut
buffer)?;

        if bytes_read == 0 {

            break; // End of file

        }


        // Process the audio data in the buffer
(e.g., send it to the audio output)
```

```rust
        println!("Processing {} bytes of audio
data", bytes_read);



        // Simulate some processing time


std::thread::sleep(std::time::Duration::from_mill
is(10));


    }



    Ok(())


}



fn main() -> Result<(), Box<dyn
std::error::Error>> {

    stream_audio("my_music.ogg", 1024)?; //
Stream in 1KB chunks

    Ok(())


}
```

This example shows how to read an audio file in chunks. In a real
game, you would replace the println! and std::thread::sleep with

code that sends the audio data to the audio output device using your chosen audio library.

Exercise:

1. Explain the trade-offs between using uncompressed and compressed audio file formats in games, providing specific examples of when each format would be appropriate.
2. Describe how sound caching can improve audio playback performance and discuss the potential limitations of caching.
3. Explain the concept of voice limiting and its importance in preventing audio overload, providing a real-world scenario in a game where voice limiting would be necessary.
4. Write a simple Rust function that simulates audio streaming by reading a file in chunks and processing each chunk (you can use a placeholder for the actual audio output).
5. Research and describe a game that effectively utilizes audio optimization techniques, explaining which techniques are likely being used and how they contribute to the overall audio experience and game performance.
6. Extend the Rodio example from the previous section to implement basic sound caching for frequently played sound effects, measuring the performance improvement (e.g., by timing the playback).

Chapter 8: User Interface Design

Okay, let's talk about user interface (UI) design in games. This is a really crucial area, because the UI is often the player's primary way of interacting with your game. A well-designed UI can make a game intuitive and enjoyable, while a poorly designed one can lead to frustration and confusion.

This chapter will cover the key aspects of UI design, from making UIs feel responsive to ensuring they're accessible to everyone.

8.1 Creating Responsive User Interfaces

Okay, let's talk about making UIs that feel great to use in games. This is all about creating a sense of immediacy and control for the player. A responsive UI is one that reacts to their actions in a way that feels smooth, predictable, and satisfying. It's a subtle but really important aspect of game feel.

When we say a UI is "responsive," we're talking about how quickly and clearly it reacts to player input. It's about avoiding any sense of lag or delay that can make the player feel disconnected from the game.

Here's a detailed exploration of what makes a UI responsive:

1. Immediate Feedback: The Instant Reaction

The most fundamental aspect of responsiveness is providing immediate feedback whenever the player interacts with a UI element. This feedback lets the player know that their action has been registered and that the UI is acknowledging their input.

What it is:

- It's the UI's way of saying, "Gotcha! I heard you!"
- It's about providing a clear and unambiguous response to every action.

Forms of Feedback:

- Visual Changes: This is the most common type of feedback. When a button is clicked, it might:
  - Highlight or change color.
  - Appear to depress or animate slightly.
  - Display a ripple effect.

Sound Effects: A subtle click, pop, or confirmation sound can provide auditory feedback.

Haptic Feedback: If the player is using a controller, a brief vibration can enhance the sense of interaction.

Cursor Changes: The mouse cursor might change shape to indicate that an element is clickable or that an action is in progress.

Why it's important:

- Reduces uncertainty: The player is never left wondering if their click was missed or if the UI is frozen.

- Enhances the feeling of control: It makes the player feel like they're directly manipulating the UI.
- Improves overall user experience: A snappy, responsive UI is simply more pleasant to use.

Real-world example:

- Think about the buttons on your smartphone. When you tap one, it usually highlights instantly. This immediate visual feedback makes the phone feel responsive.

2. Smooth Animations: Fluid Transitions

If your UI uses animations (which is often the case for things like menus appearing or elements transitioning), those animations need to be smooth and fluid.

What it is:

- Animations should flow seamlessly from one state to another, without any stuttering or jerkiness.
- This is about creating a sense of polish and visual appeal.

Factors for Smoothness:

- Frame Rate: The animation must be rendered at a high enough frame rate (e.g., 60 frames per second) to appear smooth.
- Efficient Rendering: The UI elements being animated should be drawn efficiently to avoid overloading the GPU.

- Easing: The animation's speed should change over time (e.g., accelerating at the start and decelerating at the end) to create a more natural and pleasing effect.

Why it's important:

- Improves visual appeal: Smooth animations look more professional and polished.
- Enhances immersion: Fluid transitions can contribute to a more seamless and engaging experience.
- Reduces eye strain: Choppy animations can be visually distracting and even cause discomfort.

Real-world example:

- The way windows and apps slide in and out on a modern operating system is a good example of smooth UI animation.

3. Consistent Performance: Stability Under Pressure

A responsive UI needs to maintain its responsiveness even when the game is under stress. If the UI becomes sluggish or unresponsive when the game is loading or during intense gameplay, it can be very frustrating for the player.

What it is:

- The UI should maintain a consistent frame rate and respond to input without noticeable delays, regardless of the game's overall performance.

Achieving Consistent Performance:

- UI Threading: In some cases, it might be necessary to run the UI on a separate thread to ensure it doesn't get blocked by other game processes.
- Optimized Rendering: UI elements should be drawn efficiently to minimize their impact on the GPU.
- Input Prioritization: Input events related to the UI should be prioritized over other game events to ensure they're handled promptly.

Why it's important:

- Maintains a feeling of control: The player always feels like they're directly interacting with the UI.
- Avoids frustration: Unresponsive UIs can be incredibly annoying and can detract from the overall game experience.

Real-world example:

- Think about a complex strategy game with lots of units on the screen. The UI should still be responsive even when the game is rendering all those units.

4. Clear State Changes: Visual Communication

A responsive UI also needs to communicate its current state effectively. The player should always be able to easily understand which elements are:

- Selected: The element the player is currently focused on.
- Active: The element that is currently performing an action.

- Disabled: The element that cannot be interacted with.

How to achieve this:

- Color and Style: Use different colors, fonts, and styles to distinguish between different states.
- Highlighting and Dimming: Highlight selected or active elements and dim or gray out disabled elements.
- Animations: Use subtle animations to indicate state changes.
- Tooltips and Labels: Provide clear labels and tooltips to explain the function and state of UI elements.

Why it's important:

- Reduces confusion: The player always knows what's going on with the UI.
- Improves usability: It's easier for the player to navigate and interact with the UI.

Real-world example:

- Consider the buttons on a website. Selected buttons might have a different background color, while disabled buttons might be grayed out and non-clickable.

5. Input Handling: Adapting to Different Controls

A responsive UI needs to handle input from various devices (mouse, keyboard, gamepad, touchscreens) in a consistent and predictable way.

What it is:

- The UI should respond to input in a way that feels natural for each device.
- Controls should be intuitive and easy to learn.

Key aspects:

- Accurate Hit Detection: The UI should accurately determine which element the player is interacting with.
- Intuitive Navigation: Players should be able to move between UI elements easily using the keyboard or gamepad.
- Context-Sensitive Controls: The UI might provide different actions depending on the current context (e.g., right-clicking might open a context menu).

Why it's important:

- Provides a consistent experience: The UI should feel good to use regardless of the input device.
- Increases accessibility: It allows players with different preferences or needs to control the game effectively.

Real-world example:

- Consider a video game menu. Players should be able to navigate it using the arrow keys on a keyboard, the D-pad on a gamepad, or by tapping on the screen.

By paying attention to these details, you can create a responsive UI that enhances the player's experience and makes your game feel polished and professional.

8.2 Integrating UI Libraries with Rust Game Engines

Okay, let's talk about how we actually build those user interfaces in our Rust games. We rarely create every single button, menu, and text box from scratch. Instead, we use UI libraries that provide pre-built components and tools, saving us a lot of time and effort.

UI libraries are like toolboxes specifically designed for creating user interfaces. They give you the basic building blocks and the mechanisms to arrange them and make them interactive.

Here's a breakdown of what's involved in integrating these libraries into your Rust game engine:

1. Choosing a UI Library: Picking the Right Tools

The first step is selecting a UI library that fits your project's needs. There are several options available in the Rust ecosystem, and each has its own strengths and weaknesses.

Iced:

- A cross-platform GUI library focused on simplicity and ease of use. It's designed to be relatively straightforward to learn and use, making it a good choice for projects that don't require highly complex or heavily customized UIs.

Strengths:

- Relatively simple API.
- Cross-platform support (works on desktop and web).
- Uses a reactive architecture, which can make UI updates efficient.

Considerations:

- Might not be as flexible or performant as some other options for very demanding UIs.

Egui:

- An immediate mode GUI library that emphasizes performance and flexibility. Immediate mode GUIs work by redrawing the UI every frame, which can be very efficient if done correctly.

Strengths:

- High performance, making it suitable for in-game tools and editors.
- Highly flexible and customizable.
- Works well with game engines.

Considerations:

- The immediate mode paradigm can have a steeper learning curve than retained mode GUIs (like Iced).

Nuklear:

- Another immediate mode GUI library, Nuklear is designed to be very lightweight and fast. It's often used in embedded systems or games where performance is absolutely critical.

Strengths:

- Extremely lightweight and fast.
- Small memory footprint.

Considerations:

- Might have a less feature-rich set of UI components compared to Iced or Egui.

Other Options:

- There might be other UI libraries or approaches, but Iced, Egui, and Nuklear are some of the more commonly considered ones in the Rust game development space.

The choice of UI library depends on factors such as:

- UI Complexity: How complex will your UI be? Simple menus or elaborate in-game interfaces?
- Performance Requirements: Does your UI need to be extremely fast, or is responsiveness the primary concern?
- Platform Support: Does the library work on all your target platforms (desktop, web, mobile)?
- Rendering Integration: How easily can the library be integrated with your game's rendering system?
- Ease of Use: How easy is it to learn and use the library's API?

2. Rendering the UI: Getting It on Screen

UI libraries provide functions or methods for drawing UI elements to the screen. You'll need to integrate these with your game's rendering process. This can involve several steps:

- Creating UI Textures: Many libraries require you to create textures to display text, images, and other UI elements. You might need to manage these textures and update them when the UI changes.
- Using Shaders (GPU Rendering): For more complex UIs, you might use shaders (programs that run on the GPU) to render the UI. This can improve performance, especially for animations and effects.
- Drawing on Top of the Game Scene: You'll typically want to render the UI on top of the main game scene so that it's always visible. This might involve using a separate rendering pass or a different camera.

3. Handling Input: Making It Interactive

You'll need to capture input events (mouse clicks, key presses, touch events) and pass them to the UI library. The library will then determine which UI element was interacted with and trigger the appropriate actions.

- Event Handling: UI libraries often use an event-driven system. This means that your game code provides functions (event handlers) that are called when specific UI events occur (e.g., a button is clicked).
- Input Mapping: You might need to map input events to UI actions. For example, pressing the "Enter" key might be equivalent to clicking a "Submit" button.
- Focus Management: The UI library needs to manage focus, determining which UI element is currently active and receiving input.

4. Layout and Styling: Arranging and Making It Look Good

UI libraries provide tools for arranging UI elements on the screen and controlling their appearance.

Layout:

- UI libraries offer various layout systems:
    - Absolute Positioning: Placing elements at specific coordinates.
    - Relative Positioning: Placing elements relative to each other.
    - Layout Containers: Using grids, rows, and columns to automatically arrange elements.
    - Layout Algorithms: More sophisticated algorithms that automatically adjust the layout based on screen size and content.

Styling:

- UI libraries allow you to customize the appearance of UI elements:
  - Colors (background, text, borders).
  - Fonts (size, style, weight).
  - Padding and margins (spacing).
  - Borders and outlines.
  - Effects (shadows, gradients).

Example: Conceptual UI Integration

It's difficult to give a concise and complete example without picking a specific UI library and a game engine. However, here's a conceptual snippet to illustrate the basic idea:

Rust

```rust
// (Hypothetical example - this is not
functional code)


struct Game {


    // ... game state


    ui_manager: UIManager, // Some UI
management system


    // ... rendering system
```

```rust
}

impl Game {

    fn new() -> Self {

        Game {

            // ... initialize game
state

            ui_manager:
UIManager::new(),

            // ... initialize rendering
system

        }

    }

    fn handle_input(&mut self, input:
InputEvent) {

        // Pass input to the UI manager
```

```rust
        self.ui_manager.handle_input(input);


        // ... handle other game input

    }


    fn update(&mut self, delta_time:
f32) {

        // ... update game logic



        // Update the UI


self.ui_manager.update(delta_time);

    }


    fn render(&mut self) {

        // ... render game scene
```

```rust
        // Render the UI

        self.ui_manager.render();

    }

}

struct UIManager {

    // ... UI data and logic (e.g.,
using a UI library)

}

impl UIManager {

    fn new() -> Self {

        // ... initialize UI

        UIManager { /* ... */ }

    }
```

```rust
    fn handle_input(&mut self, input:
InputEvent) {

        // ... handle UI input

    }


    fn update(&mut self, delta_time:
f32) {

        // ... update UI animations and
logic

    }


    fn render(&mut self) {

        // ... render UI elements

    }

}


// Hypothetical InputEvent

enum InputEvent {
```

```rust
    MouseClick { x: i32, y: i32,
button: MouseButton },

    KeyPress { key: KeyCode },

    // ... other input events

}

// Hypothetical enums

enum MouseButton {

    Left, Right, Middle

}

enum KeyCode {

    Space, Enter, Escape

}

fn main() {
```

```rust
let mut game = Game::new();

// ... game loop

loop {

    // ... get input events

    let input = /* ... */;

    game.handle_input(input);

    game.update(0.016); // Example delta time

    game.render();

}

}
```

This example illustrates how a UIManager might be used to separate UI logic from the main game logic and how input and rendering are handled.

Exercise:

1. Choose a Rust UI library (Iced, Egui, or Nuklear) and explain its strengths and weaknesses in the context of game development.
2. Describe the different approaches to UI layout (absolute positioning, relative positioning, layout containers) and provide examples of when each approach would be most appropriate in a game UI.
3. Explain the challenges involved in integrating a UI library with a game engine's rendering pipeline and discuss potential solutions.
4. Design a simple UI for a game's settings menu, considering layout, styling, and input handling.
5. Research and describe how a specific game engine or game library handles UI input (e.g., mouse clicks, keyboard presses, gamepad input).
6. Implement a basic UI in Rust using your chosen UI library, including elements like buttons, text fields, and images, and demonstrate how to handle user interactions with those elements.

8.3 Accessibility Considerations

Okay, let's have a really important conversation about making our games and their user interfaces (UIs) usable by as many people as possible. This is what we mean by accessibility, and it's a crucial aspect of inclusive game development. It's about designing games that can be enjoyed by players with a wide range of abilities and disabilities.

Accessibility isn't just a "nice-to-have" feature; it's a fundamental principle of good design. It ensures that everyone has an equal opportunity to experience the joy and engagement that games can offer.

Here's a detailed look at the key accessibility considerations we should keep in mind when designing UIs:

1. Keyboard Navigation: Beyond the Mouse

Many players, for various reasons, might not be able to use a mouse or other pointing device effectively. Keyboard navigation provides an alternative way to interact with the UI.

What it is:

- It's the ability to navigate and interact with all UI elements using only the keyboard.
- This typically involves using the Tab key to move focus between elements and the Enter key to select them.
- Arrow keys might also be used for navigation within lists or menus.

Key Design Principles:

- Logical Order: The navigation order should be logical and predictable. Players should be able to easily understand where they'll go when they press Tab or an arrow key.
- Clear Focus Indication: The currently focused element should be clearly highlighted. This could be a colored border, a background change, or an animation.
- Accessibility of All Elements: Every interactive element (buttons, text fields, lists, dropdowns) must be accessible via the keyboard.
- Context-Sensitive Navigation: The keyboard controls should make sense within the current context. For example, in a text field, arrow keys should move the cursor, not navigate to other UI elements.

Real-world example:

- Think about navigating a website using only the Tab key. The focused element is usually highlighted with a blue or orange outline. This is keyboard navigation in action.

2. Screen Reader Compatibility: Making the UI Speak

Screen readers are software programs that read aloud the text and other information displayed on a computer screen. They are essential for visually impaired users.

What it is:

- Designing the UI so that screen readers can accurately interpret and convey its content.
- This involves providing semantic information about UI elements.

How to achieve it:

- Text Alternatives: Provide text alternatives (often called "alt text") for images and other non-text elements. This allows the screen reader to describe the image.
- Labels and Descriptions: Use clear and descriptive labels for buttons, text fields, and other interactive elements.
- Semantic Structure: Structure the UI in a way that makes sense to a screen reader. For example, use headings to indicate sections and lists to group related items.
- ARIA Attributes: ARIA (Accessible Rich Internet Applications) attributes can be used to provide additional information to screen readers, such as the role of an

element (e.g., "button," "listbox") and its state (e.g., "checked," "expanded").

Why it's important:

- Allows visually impaired players to access and understand the UI.
- Enables them to navigate menus, read information, and interact with the game.

Real-world example:

- Websites that are designed to be accessible use ARIA attributes and provide alt text for images to ensure screen readers can convey the content to visually impaired users.

3. Color Contrast: Readability for All

Sufficient color contrast between text and background is crucial for making the UI readable, especially for players with low vision or color blindness.

What it is:

- The difference in luminance (brightness) between the text and its background should be high enough to make the text easily distinguishable.

Guidelines:

- WCAG (Web Content Accessibility Guidelines) provide specific contrast ratios that should be met for different text sizes.
- Tools are available online to check the contrast ratio of your color combinations.
- Avoid relying solely on color to convey information. Use other visual cues like icons or text labels.

Why it's important:

- Improves readability for players with low vision.
- Ensures that players with color blindness can still distinguish between UI elements.
- Reduces eye strain.

Real-world example:

- Think about street signs. They use high contrast colors (like black text on a yellow background) to ensure they're easily readable in various lighting conditions.

4. Font Size and Style: Customization for Comfort

Allowing players to adjust the font size and choose different font styles can significantly improve readability and reduce eye strain.

What it is:

- Providing in-game options to change the size of text.

- Offering a selection of font styles (e.g., sans-serif fonts are often easier to read on screens).

Why it's important:

- Accommodates players with different visual preferences.
- Helps players with low vision to read the text.
- Reduces eye strain, especially during long gaming sessions.

Real-world example:

- Many word processors and web browsers allow users to zoom in or change the font size for better readability.

5. Subtitles and Captions: Access to Audio Information

Subtitles (for dialogue) and captions (for all relevant audio, including sound effects) are essential for players who are deaf or hard of hearing.

What they are:

- Textual representations of the audio in the game.
- Subtitles typically focus on spoken dialogue.
- Captions include dialogue, sound effects, music cues, and other relevant audio information.

Key Features:

- Clear and Accurate: The text should accurately reflect what is being said and heard.

- Synchronized: The text should be synchronized with the audio.
- Customizable: Allow players to adjust the font size, color, and background of the text.
- Placement: Place the text in a position that doesn't obscure important visual information.

Why they're important:

- Allow deaf and hard-of-hearing players to understand the game's story and audio cues.
- Can also be helpful for players in noisy environments or those who prefer to play without sound.

Real-world example:

- Think about the subtitles and captions on TV shows and movies. They make the content accessible to a wider audience.

6. Rebindable Controls: Tailoring the Experience

Allowing players to remap or rebind the controls is crucial for accessibility, especially for players with motor impairments.

What it is:

- Giving players the ability to assign different input devices or buttons to specific game actions.
- For example, a player might want to change the "jump" action from the spacebar to a different key.

Why it's important:

- Accommodates players with different physical limitations.
- Allows players to use their preferred control schemes.
- Reduces strain and discomfort.

Real-world example:

- Many PC games allow players to remap keyboard and mouse controls.

By carefully considering these accessibility factors, you can create games that are more inclusive and enjoyable for everyone. It's not just about meeting minimum requirements; it's about designing with empathy and creating experiences that celebrate diversity.

Chapter 9: Animation and Effects

Okay, let's talk about how we make our games visually exciting and dynamic. This chapter is all about animation and visual effects – the techniques that bring our characters to life and make our game worlds feel spectacular.

9.1 Advanced Animation Techniques: Skeletal Animation

Okay, let's talk about how we make characters and creatures move in 3D games. One of the most important and common techniques is called skeletal animation.[1] It's the way we give digital characters the ability to walk, run, jump, and express emotions.

Skeletal animation is a clever approach that's much more efficient and versatile than older methods, like trying to animate every single point on a 3D model.[2]

Here's a breakdown of how it works:

1. The Skeleton: The Underlying Structure

Think of a character as having an invisible skeleton inside, just like you do. This skeleton is made up of individual "bones" that are connected to each other in a hierarchical structure.[3]

Bones: These are like the rigid parts of your body.[4] In a 3D character, they are represented by mathematical objects (often matrices) that define their position, orientation, and scale.[5]

Hierarchy: The bones are arranged in a tree-like structure.

For example:

- The torso bone is the "root" or parent.

- The upper arm bones are children of the torso bone.
- The forearm bones are children of the upper arm bones.
- And so on.

This hierarchical structure is crucial because when you move a parent bone, all its child bones move along with it.[6] This is how we get natural-looking movement.

Example:

- If you rotate the torso bone, the entire character rotates.
- If you rotate the upper arm bone, the forearm and hand bones also rotate.

2. Skinning: Attaching the Model to the Bones

The 3D model of the character (the surface you actually see, the "skin") is attached to this underlying skeleton.[7] This process is called "skinning."

Vertex Weights: Each vertex (point) of the 3D model is assigned "weights."[8] These weights determine how much each bone influences the movement of that vertex.[9]

- A vertex close to the upper arm bone will have a high weight for that bone and low weights for other bones.
- A vertex on the character's hand will be strongly influenced by the hand bone and wrist bone.

Interpolation: When a bone moves, the skinning algorithm calculates the new position of each vertex by blending the influence of the bones based on their weights.

Example:

- When you bend your elbow, the skin around your elbow doesn't just snap into a new position. It smoothly deforms. Skinning simulates this by having the vertices in that area influenced by both the upper arm and forearm bones.

3. Animation: Bringing the Skeleton to Life

To animate the character, we don't directly manipulate the vertices of the 3D model. Instead, we animate the bones of the skeleton.

- Keyframes: Animators create "keyframes," which are snapshots of the skeleton's pose at specific points in time.[10]
- Interpolation: The computer then smoothly interpolates (blends) between these keyframes to create the animation.[11]
- Animation Data: The animation data stores the rotation, translation (movement), and scale of each bone over time.[12]

Example:

- To make a character walk, the animator creates keyframes for poses like:
    - Leg forward, arm back.
    - Leg straight, arm at rest.
    - Leg back, arm forward.
- The computer then smoothly transitions between these poses.[13]

Why is Skeletal Animation So Important?

- Efficiency: It's much more efficient than animating every vertex individually. You only need to animate the relatively small number of bones.

- Realistic Deformations: Skinning allows for natural-looking bending and stretching of the character's skin.
- Reusability: You can easily apply different animations to the same skeleton. For example, you can have a "walk" animation, a "run" animation, and an "attack" animation, all played on the same character.
- Control: Animators have precise control over the character's movement.[14]

Real-world Examples:

- Virtually every modern 3D game uses skeletal animation for characters, creatures, and even some objects.
- Think about the way characters move in action games, the facial expressions in RPGs, or the way creatures behave in fantasy games. All of this is made possible by skeletal animation.

Conceptual Rust Example:

It's challenging to provide a fully functional skeletal animation example without a specific rendering library or game engine. However, here's a simplified conceptual example in Rust to illustrate the core principles:

```rust
use std::collections::HashMap;

#[derive(Debug, Copy, Clone)]

struct Mat4 {

    // A 4x4 matrix (used for transformations)
```

```rust
    data: [[f32; 4]; 4],

}

#[derive(Debug, Copy, Clone)]

struct Vec3 {

    // A 3D vector

    x: f32,

    y: f32,

    z: f32,

}

#[derive(Debug, Copy, Clone)]

struct Bone {

    name: String,

    parent: Option<String>, // Name of the
parent bone

    transform: Mat4,        // Local
transformation (relative to parent)

}

struct Skeleton {
```

```rust
    bones: HashMap<String, Bone>,

    root_bones: Vec<String>, // Names of the
root bones

}

impl Skeleton {

    fn new() -> Self {

        Skeleton {

            bones: HashMap::new(),

            root_bones: Vec::new(),

        }

    }

    fn add_bone(&mut self, bone: Bone) {

        if bone.parent.is_none() {

self.root_bones.push(bone.name.clone());

        }

        self.bones.insert(bone.name.clone(),
bone);
```

```rust
    }

    // (Simplified) Calculate the global
transform of a bone

    fn get_global_transform(&self,
bone_name: &str) -> Mat4 {

        let mut global_transform = Mat4 {

            data: [

                [1.0, 0.0, 0.0, 0.0],

                [0.0, 1.0, 0.0, 0.0],

                [0.0, 0.0, 1.0, 0.0],

                [0.0, 0.0, 0.0, 1.0],

            ],

        }; // Identity matrix


        let mut current_bone_name =
Some(bone_name.to_string());


    while let Some(name) = current_bone_name
{
```

```rust
            if let Some(bone) =
self.bones.get(&name) {

                // (Matrix multiplication
logic would go here)

                // global_transform =
bone.transform global_transform;

                current_bone_name =
bone.parent.clone();

        } else {

            break;

        }

    }

    global_transform

}

// (Animation playback logic would go
here)

}

// (Skinning data and rendering logic would
go here)

fn main() {
```

```rust
    let mut skeleton = Skeleton::new();

    skeleton.add_bone(Bone {

        name: "torso".to_string(),

        parent: None,

        transform: Mat4 { data: [ /* ... */
] },

    });

    skeleton.add_bone(Bone {

        name: "upper_arm_l".to_string(),

        parent: Some("torso".to_string()),

        transform: Mat4 { data: [ /* ... */
] },

    });

    skeleton.add_bone(Bone {

        name: "forearm_l".to_string(),

        parent:
Some("upper_arm_l".to_string()),

        transform: Mat4 { data: [ /* ... */
] },
```

```
    });

    // ... add more bones

    let global_hand_transform =
skeleton.get_global_transform("forearm_l");

    println!("Global hand transform: {:?}",
global_hand_transform);

    // (Animation and rendering logic would
be more complex)

}
```

This example shows how to represent a skeleton in Rust and calculate the global transform of a bone based on the bone hierarchy.

Exercise:

1. Explain the concept of skeletal animation in your own words, emphasizing its advantages over other animation techniques for 3D characters.
2. Describe the roles of "bones," "skinning," and "vertex weights" in the skeletal animation process.
3. Provide three real-world examples of how skeletal animation is used in different types of games (e.g., fighting games, RPGs, platformers).
4. Research and explain the concept of "inverse kinematics" in skeletal animation and its benefits for creating natural and interactive character poses.
5. Design a simple bone hierarchy for a 3D character's arm, specifying the parent-child relationships between the bones.[15]

6. Extend the Rust example above to include a function that calculates the position of a vertex on the character's skin based on the influence of the bones and their weights.

9.2 Particle Systems and Visual Effects

Okay, let's talk about how we create those really cool, dynamic visual effects in games. We're going to focus on particle systems and some other related techniques that make game worlds feel alive and exciting.

Particle systems are a way of simulating a large number of tiny objects, called particles.[1] Instead of animating each of these particles individually (which would be incredibly tedious and computationally expensive), we define rules that govern their behavior. Think of it as setting up a miniature, controlled chaos.

What are Particle Systems Used For?

Particle systems are incredibly versatile and can be used to create a wide range of visual effects:[2]

- Smoke and Fire: Simulating the swirling patterns of smoke or the flickering and dancing of flames.[3]
- Explosions: Generating debris, shockwaves, and the fiery aftermath of explosions.[4]
- Rain and Snow: Creating the effect of falling precipitation.[5]
- Magic Effects: Visualizing magical spells, energy fields, or mystical auras.[6]
- Environmental Effects: Simulating dust motes in the air, leaves blowing in the wind, or water splashes.[7]

Key Components of a Particle System

To understand how particle systems work, let's break down their key components:

Particle: A single instance of the small object being simulated.

Each particle has properties like:

- Position: Its location in 3D space.
- Velocity: Its speed and direction of movement.
- Color: Its color.
- Size: Its dimensions.
- Lifetime: How long it exists before disappearing.

Emitter: The source that generates new particles. The emitter can have properties like:

- Emission Rate: How many particles are created per second.
- Emission Shape: The area or volume from which particles are emitted (e.g., a point, a sphere, a plane).
- Particle Properties: The initial values for position, velocity, color, etc., of the emitted particles.

Motion Rules: These rules govern how particles move and change over time. Common motion rules include:

- Gravity: Simulating the force of gravity pulling particles downwards.
- Wind: Simulating the effect of wind on particle movement.[8]
- Drag: Simulating air resistance.[9]
- Velocity Changes: Modifying the particle's velocity over time.[10]

Appearance Rules: These rules control how particles look.[11]

- Color Changes: Animating the particle's color over its lifetime (e.g., fading from bright to dark).[12]
- Size Changes: Animating the particle's size (e.g., growing or shrinking).[13]
- Texture: Applying a small image (texture) to the particle.

Lifetime Rules: These rules determine how long particles exist.[14]

- Fixed Lifetime: Each particle exists for a specific duration.[15]
- Random Lifetime: Each particle has a random lifetime within a range.

Example: A Simplified Particle System in Rust (Conceptual)

It's tricky to provide a fully functional and renderable particle system example without relying on a specific game engine or rendering library. However, here's a conceptual snippet in Rust to illustrate the core principles:

Rust

```
use std::collections::VecDeque;

use std::time::{Duration, Instant};

struct Particle {

    position: [f32; 3], // 3D position (x, y, z)
```

```rust
    velocity: [f32; 3], // 3D velocity
(direction and speed)

    color: [f32; 4],     // RGBA color (red,
green, blue, alpha)

    size: f32,

    lifetime: f32,     // How long the
particle lasts

}

struct ParticleSystem {

    particles: VecDeque<Particle>, // Using
a deque for efficient removal

    emission_rate: f32,     // Particles
emitted per second

    last_emission_time: Instant,

}

impl ParticleSystem {

    fn new(emission_rate: f32) -> Self {

        ParticleSystem {

            particles: VecDeque::new(),

            emission_rate,
```

```rust
            last_emission_time:
Instant::now(),

        }

    }    .

    fn emit(&mut self, position: [f32; 3],
color: [f32; 4], current_time: Instant) {

        let time_since_last_emission =
current_time.duration_since(self.last_emissi
on_time).as_secs_f32();

        let particles_to_emit =
(time_since_last_emission *
self.emission_rate) as usize;

        for _ in 0..particles_to_emit {

            let particle = Particle {

                position,

                velocity: [

                    (rand::random::<f32>() -
0.5) * 2.0, // Random x velocity

                    1.0,
// Upward y velocity

                    (rand::random::<f32>() -
0.5) * 2.0,  // Random z velocity
```

```
                ],

                color,

                size: 0.1,

                lifetime: 1.0, // Lasts for
1 second

            };


self.particles.push_back(particle);

        }

        self.last_emission_time =
current_time;

    }

    fn update(&mut self, delta_time: f32) {

        // Update particle positions,
colors, lifetimes, etc.

        for particle in &mut self.particles
{

            particle.position[0] +=
particle.velocity[0] * delta_time;

            particle.position[1] +=
particle.velocity[1] * delta_time;
```

```rust
            particle.position[2] +=
particle.velocity[2] * delta_time;

            particle.lifetime -= delta_time;

            // Simple color fading

            particle.color[3] =
particle.lifetime.clamp(0.0, 1.0); // Alpha
fades over lifetime

        }



        // Remove dead particles (particles
with lifetime <= 0)

        self.particles.retain(|p| p.lifetime
> 0.0);

    }



    fn render(&self) {

        // (Rendering logic would go here,
using a graphics library)

        // This is a placeholder for
actually drawing the particles on screen

        for particle in &self.particles {
```

```rust
        println!("Rendering particle at:
{:?}, color: {:?}", particle.position,
particle.color);

        }

    }

}

fn main() {

    let mut system =
ParticleSystem::new(50.0); // Emit 50
particles per second

    let start_time = Instant::now();

    // Simulate for a few frames

    for i in 0..10 {

        let current_time = Instant::now();

        system.emit([0.0, 0.0, 0.0], [1.0,
0.0, 0.0, 1.0], current_time); // Emit red
particles

        system.emit([0.5, 0.0, 0.0], [0.0,
1.0, 0.0, 1.0], current_time); // Emit green
particles

        system.update(0.1); // Simulate 0.1
seconds
```

```
        system.render();


    std::thread::sleep(Duration::from_millis(100
    )); // Simulate frame delay


        }


    }
```

This example shows the basic structure of a particle system, including emission, updating particle properties, and rudimentary rendering.

Beyond Particle Systems: Other Visual Effects

Visual effects (VFX) in games go beyond just particle systems. Here are some other important techniques:

Lighting Effects:

- Creating realistic or stylized lighting is crucial.

Examples:

- Lens Flares: Simulating the scattering of light within a camera lens.
- God Rays: Beams of light shining through dust or fog.
- Light Shafts: Similar to god rays but often more focused.

Distortion Effects:

- Warping the rendered image to create effects like:
    - Heat haze (simulating the shimmering effect of hot air).[16]
    - Shockwaves (visualizing the pressure wave from an explosion).[17]
    - Magical distortions.

Post-Processing Effects:

- Applying effects to the entire rendered image after the scene has been drawn.

Examples:

- Bloom: Creating a glowing effect around bright objects.
- Motion Blur: Simulating the blurring of moving objects.[18]
- Color Grading: Adjusting the overall color and tone of the image.

Exercise:

1. Explain the concept of a particle system in your own words and describe the different types of visual effects it can be used to create in games.
2. Describe the key components of a particle system, including emission, motion rules, appearance rules, and lifetime rules, and explain how each component contributes to the overall visual effect.

3. Provide three real-world examples of how particle systems are used in different game genres to enhance the visual experience and convey information to the player.
4. Research and describe a specific technique for creating a visual effect in games, such as fluid simulation or procedural animation, and explain its applications and benefits.
5. Design a particle system for a specific effect in a game, such as a magic spell or a dust storm, and describe the parameters you would use to control its behavior and achieve the desired visual result.
6. Extend the simplified particle system example above to include more realistic particle motion, such as gravity and drag, and implement a simple color fading effect to make particles gradually disappear over their lifetime.

9.3 Creating Engaging Game Experiences

Okay, let's talk about how animation and visual effects go beyond just looking good; they're powerful tools for making games more engaging and impactful.

We often think of animation and effects as primarily visual, but they have a profound effect on how a game feels and how players interact with it. They can communicate information, emphasize key moments, and even influence the player's emotions.

Here's how animation and effects contribute to creating engaging game experiences:

1. Feedback and Communication: Showing and Telling

Animation and effects are excellent ways to provide feedback to the player and communicate information about what's happening in the game.

Character State: A character's animations can clearly indicate their current state:

- Are they attacking?
- Are they dodging?
- Are they injured?
- Are they interacting with an object?

Gameplay Information: Visual effects can convey critical information about gameplay:

- The area of effect of a spell.
- The amount of damage dealt.
- The direction of an attack.
- The status of an enemy (e.g., poisoned, stunned).

Example:

- In a fighting game, a character's attack animation isn't just about looking cool; it also tells the player when the attack will hit and how much range it has.
- A flashing effect on an enemy might indicate that they are vulnerable to a critical hit.

2. Emphasis and Focus: Guiding the Player's Attention

Effects can be used to draw the player's attention to important elements or events in the game world. This is crucial for guiding the player's focus and preventing them from missing critical information.

Highlighting Objects:

- Particle effects, glowing outlines, or other visual cues can highlight objects that the player can interact with.

Signaling Events:

- Effects can signal important events, such as a door opening, an enemy spawning, or a puzzle being solved.

Directing the Player:

- Visual effects can be used to direct the player's gaze towards a specific location or path.

Example:

- In an adventure game, a shimmering particle effect might draw the player's attention to a hidden object.
- A dramatic camera shake and explosion effect can emphasize a critical moment in the story.

3. Emotional Impact: Setting the Tone

Animation and effects can be powerful tools for evoking emotions and creating a specific mood or atmosphere in your game.

Excitement and Action:

- Fast-paced animations and explosive effects can create a sense of excitement and adrenaline.

Drama and Tension:

- Slow-motion effects can emphasize dramatic moments and heighten tension.

Fear and Horror:

- Distorted visuals and unsettling sound effects can create a sense of fear and unease.

Beauty and Wonder:

- Beautifully crafted animations and particle effects can create a sense of wonder and awe.

Example:

- The use of slow motion in action games can make powerful attacks feel more impactful.
- Particle effects that swirl and change color can create a sense of magic or the supernatural.

4. Gameplay Mechanics: Integrated Design

In some cases, animation and effects are directly tied to the core gameplay mechanics of a game.

Timing and Feedback:

- A character's attack animation might determine the timing and range of their hit, providing feedback to the player about when and where they can strike.

Spatial Awareness:

- Visual effects can indicate the area of effect of a spell or ability, helping players understand its range and impact.

Gameplay Cues:

- Animations and effects can provide cues about enemy behavior or environmental hazards.

Example:

- In a rhythm game, the animations of characters might be synchronized with the music, creating a visual and auditory experience that's tightly integrated.
- In a platformer, the character's jump animation might communicate how high and far they can jump.

Example: A Simple Animation-Driven Attack (Conceptual)

To illustrate how animation can be tied to gameplay, let's consider a simplified example of an attack in a game:

Rust

```rust
struct Character {

    position: [f32; 2], // 2D position (x, y)

    animation_frame: usize,

    attack_animation: Vec<AttackFrame>,

    is_attacking: bool,

}




struct AttackFrame {

    hitbox: Option<Hitbox>, // Hitbox for this
frame (None if no hit)

    duration: f32,        // Duration of this
frame

}
```

```rust
struct Hitbox {

    offset: [f32; 2],  // Offset from character's
position

    size: [f32; 2],    // Size of the hitbox

}



impl Character {

    fn new() -> Self {

        Character {

            position: [0.0, 0.0],

            animation_frame: 0,

            attack_animation: vec![

                AttackFrame {

                    hitbox: None, // No hit on
the first frame

                    duration: 0.2,

                },

                AttackFrame {
```

```rust
                hitbox: Some(Hitbox {

                    offset: [1.0, 0.0],

                    size: [1.0, 1.0],

                }),

                duration: 0.1,

            },

        AttackFrame {

            hitbox: None, // Hit ends

            duration: 0.3,

        },

    ],

    is_attacking: false,

    }

}


fn start_attack(&mut self) {

    self.is_attacking = true;
```

```rust
        self.animation_frame = 0;

    }


    fn update(&mut self, delta_time: f32) {

        if self.is_attacking {

            // Update animation

            self.animation_frame =
(self.animation_frame + 1) %
self.attack_animation.len();


            // Check for hit

            if let Some(hitbox) =
&self.attack_animation[self.animation_frame].hitb
ox {

                // (Collision detection logic
would go here)

                println!("Attack hit! (Frame
{})", self.animation_frame);

            }
```

```rust
            // Check if animation is finished

        if self.animation_frame == 0 {

            self.is_attacking = false;

        }

    }


    fn render(&self) {

        // (Rendering logic would go here)

        println!("Character at: {:?}",
self.position);

        if self.is_attacking {

            println!("Playing attack animation
(Frame {})", self.animation_frame);

        }

    }

}
```

```rust
fn main() {

    let mut character = Character::new();



    // Simulate an attack

    character.start_attack();



    // Simulate game frames

    for _ in 0..10 {

        character.update(0.1); // Simulate 0.1
seconds per frame

        character.render();


std::thread::sleep(std::time::Duration::from_mill
is(100)); // Simulate frame delay

    }

}
```

This example shows how an attack animation can define when and where a hitbox is active, directly affecting gameplay.

Exercise:

1. Explain how animation and visual effects can be used to provide feedback to the player about their actions and the state of the game world.

2. Describe how visual effects can be used to emphasize important events or objects in a game, and provide examples from different game genres.

3. Discuss how animation and effects can be used to evoke specific emotions in players and create a desired atmosphere in a game.

4. Research and describe a specific animation technique, such as facial animation or procedural animation, and explain its applications and benefits in game development.

5. Design a sequence of animations and effects for a specific gameplay scenario, such as a character casting a spell or a vehicle transforming, and explain how these visuals would enhance the player's understanding and enjoyment of the event.

6. Extend the simplified animation-driven attack example above to include more realistic animation timing and movement, and implement a basic collision detection system to determine when the attack hits an enemy.

Chapter 10: Game Networking (Optional)

Okay, let's talk about connecting players and creating those awesome multiplayer experiences. This chapter (which we're marking as "optional" because networking can be a big and complex topic) will cover the basics of network programming with Rust and some of the key hurdles you'll face when trying to build games with low latency.

10.1 Network Programming with Rust

Network programming might seem complex, but at its core, it's about sending and receiving data between different computers. Rust provides us with some excellent tools to do this in a safe and efficient way.

Here's a breakdown of the key concepts:

1. Sockets: The Communication Points

Think of a socket as the "plug" and "socket" that you use to connect devices to a network. It's the point where a program can send and receive data.

What they are:

- A socket is essentially an endpoint for communication. It's a combination of an IP address and a port number.
  - An IP address identifies a specific device on the network (like a computer or a server).
  - A port number identifies a specific application or service running on that device. It's like an "extension" on a phone line, allowing different

programs on the same computer to communicate independently.

- Sockets can be used for communication between processes on the same machine (for example, two programs on your own computer talking to each other) or, more importantly for games, between processes on different machines connected by a network (like players on different computers playing online).

Rust's std::net **module:**

- Rust's standard library provides the std::net module, which offers the tools you need to create and work with sockets.
- This module includes structures and functions for:
  - Creating sockets (both TCP and UDP).
  - Binding sockets to specific addresses and ports.
  - Connecting to remote sockets.
  - Sending and receiving data.

Analogy:

- A good analogy for a socket is a phone.
  - The IP address is like the area code and phone number, uniquely identifying a specific phone.
  - The port number is like the extension number, allowing you to reach a specific person or department within that office.

2. TCP vs. UDP: Two Ways to Send Data

There are two main protocols that we use to send data over networks: TCP and UDP. They work in fundamentally different ways, and each has its own strengths and weaknesses.

TCP (Transmission Control Protocol):

- Connection-Oriented: TCP is a connection-oriented protocol. This means that before any data is sent, a reliable connection must be established between the sender and the receiver. It's like making a phone call: you dial the number, the other person answers, and then you start talking.
- Reliable Delivery: TCP guarantees that data will arrive at the receiver in the same order it was sent and without any errors. If a piece of data gets lost or corrupted, TCP will automatically retransmit it until it's successfully received.
- Flow Control: TCP also includes flow control mechanisms to prevent the sender from overwhelming the receiver with too much data.

Use Cases in Games:

- TCP is generally preferred for data that *must* be delivered reliably and in the correct sequence, such as:
    - Player movement updates (ensuring everyone sees the accurate positions of other players).
    - Game state updates (e.g., changes to scores, inventory, or game rules).
    - Chat messages (so players can communicate without missing parts of messages).

UDP (User Datagram Protocol):

- Connectionless: UDP is a connectionless protocol. This means that data is sent in packets (called datagrams) without establishing a connection first. It's like sending a postcard: you write your message, address it, and drop it in the mail. There's no guarantee that it will arrive, or that it will arrive in the order you sent it.
- Unreliable Delivery: UDP does not guarantee delivery or ordering. Packets can be lost, corrupted, or arrive out of order.
- Lower Overhead: UDP is generally faster than TCP because it doesn't have the overhead of establishing a connection, error checking, and flow control.

Use Cases in Games:

- UDP is often used for data where occasional loss is acceptable and speed is more important than perfect accuracy, such as:
  - Real-time voice or video streaming (where a few lost packets might cause a brief glitch but won't ruin the overall experience).
  - Game updates where the latest information is more important than old, accurate information (e.g., sending player positions every frame; if a position update is lost, the next one will likely arrive soon after).

Choosing between TCP and UDP:

- Games often use a combination of both protocols to handle different types of network traffic.

4. Asynchronous I/O: Avoiding the Wait

Network operations (sending and receiving data) can sometimes take a significant amount of time, especially over slow or congested networks. If your game code waits for these operations to complete before continuing, it can freeze or become unresponsive.

Asynchronous I/O (or Async I/O) provides a way to perform network operations without blocking the main thread of your game.

How it works:

- Instead of waiting for a network operation to finish, your code starts the operation and then continues executing other tasks.
- When the network operation is complete, your code is notified, and it can then process the result.

Rust's async **and** await**:**

- Rust provides the async and await keywords to make asynchronous programming easier and more efficient.
- Libraries like tokio provide a runtime environment for executing asynchronous tasks.

Benefits:

- Prevents your game from freezing or becoming unresponsive while waiting for network operations.
- Improves responsiveness and overall performance, especially in networked games where latency is a major concern.

5. Serialization: Converting Game Data

Game data (like player positions, game state, etc.) needs to be converted into a format that can be sent over the network. This process is called serialization. It's like translating a complex data structure (that your program understands) into a sequence of bytes (that can be transmitted).

On the receiving end, the data needs to be converted back into its original format. This is called deserialization.

Serialization Formats:

- Common serialization formats include:
    - JSON (human-readable, but less efficient in terms of size)
    - Binary formats (more efficient in terms of size and speed, but less human-readable)

Rust Libraries:

- Rust libraries like serde can automate much of the serialization and deserialization process, making it much less tedious and error-prone.

Conceptual Rust Example (TCP Server)

Here's a simplified example of a basic TCP server in Rust. Keep in mind that a real-world game server would be much more complex and would likely involve asynchronous I/O and more sophisticated data handling.

Rust

```rust
use std::net::TcpListener;

use std::io::{Read, Write};

fn main() -> std::io::Result<()> {

    // Start a TCP listener on a specific
address and port

    let listener =
TcpListener::bind("127.0.0.1:8080")?; //
127.0.0.1 is the local machine (localhost),
8080 is a common port

    println!("Server listening on port
8080");




    // Accept incoming connections

    for stream in listener.incoming() { //
This loop will wait for clients to connect

        match stream {
```

```rust
        Ok(mut stream) => { // Handle
potential errors when a client tries to
connect

            println!("Connection
established!");



            // Read data from the client

            let mut buffer = [0; 1024];
// Create a buffer to store incoming data
(1024 bytes)

            match stream.read(&mut
buffer) {

                Ok(bytes_read) => {

                    let message =
String::from_utf8_lossy(&buffer[..bytes_read
]); // Convert the bytes to a String (lossy
to handle potential encoding issues)

                    println!("Received:
{}", message);



                    // Send data back to
the client
```

```rust
                    let response =
"Hello from server!\n"; // The message we'll
send back


stream.write(response.as_bytes())?; // Write
the response as bytes to the client

                        stream.flush()?; //
Ensure data is sent immediately

                    }

                    Err(e) => {

                        eprintln!("Error
reading from client: {}", e);

                    }

                }

            }

        Err(e) => {

            eprintln!("Error
establishing connection: {}", e);

            }

        }

    }
```

```
        Ok ( ( ) )

    }
```

This example demonstrates a basic TCP server that:

1. Listens for incoming connections on a specified port.
2. Accepts a connection from a client.
3. Reads data from the client.
4. Sends a response back to the client.

Exercise:

1. Explain the key differences between TCP and UDP, providing specific examples of when each protocol would be most suitable for use in a multiplayer game.
2. Describe the purpose of sockets in network programming and explain how they are used to establish communication between different computers or processes.
3. Write a simple TCP client in Rust that can connect to a server, send a message, and receive a response, including basic error handling.
4. Explain the concept of asynchronous I/O and discuss its benefits for improving the performance and responsiveness of networked games, especially when dealing with potentially slow network operations.
5. Research and describe a common serialization format used in game networking (e.g., JSON, Protocol Buffers) and explain why serialization is necessary for transmitting game data over a network.
6. Extend the TCP server example above to handle multiple clients concurrently, using either threads or asynchronous programming techniques, and explain the challenges involved in managing concurrent connections.

10.2 Low-Latency Multiplayer Games

Latency, in simple terms, is the delay between a player's action and the game's response to that action. In a single-player game, latency is primarily a matter of how fast your computer can process input and render the scene. But in a multiplayer game, network communication adds another layer of complexity.

High latency in a multiplayer game can lead to:

- Unresponsiveness: Actions feel delayed, making the game feel sluggish and frustrating.
- Inaccuracy: It becomes difficult to aim and time actions precisely.
- Unfairness: Players with lower latency have a significant advantage.

So, achieving low latency is a key goal for multiplayer game developers. Here's a breakdown of the challenges and techniques involved:

1. Network Conditions: The Unpredictable Enemy

One of the biggest hurdles is that network latency is heavily influenced by factors outside of the game developer's direct control.

- Distance: The physical distance between players and the game server introduces latency. Data has to travel across cables and through routers, and this takes time.
- Network Congestion: The amount of traffic on the internet or local network can cause delays. When the network is congested, data packets may be queued or dropped, requiring retransmission.
- Internet Service Provider (ISP) Quality: Different ISPs have different network infrastructures and peering arrangements, which can affect latency.

- Packet Loss: Data packets can be lost during transmission due to network errors or congestion.

Mitigation Strategies:

- Server Location: Hosting game servers in geographically central locations or close to players can reduce the distance data needs to travel.
- Network Protocols: Choosing efficient network protocols is important. UDP, while unreliable, is often preferred for real-time game data because it's faster than TCP.
- Data Minimization: Reducing the amount of data sent over the network can reduce network overhead and latency. This can involve compressing data or sending only essential updates.

2. Game State Synchronization: Keeping Everyone in Sync

In a multiplayer game, each player's computer has its own copy of the game world. It's crucial to keep these copies synchronized so that everyone sees a consistent version of the game.

The Problem:

- Network latency means that updates from the server take time to reach clients.
- If we simply wait for the server's update before displaying changes to the player, the game will feel laggy.

Solutions:

- Client-Side Prediction:

- The client predicts the player's movement and actions locally. This allows the player to see immediate feedback, even before the server's authoritative update arrives.
- Think of it like this: If you press the forward button, your character starts moving forward instantly on your screen, even though the server hasn't confirmed that you actually moved.

Server Reconciliation:

- The server periodically sends the authoritative game state to the clients.
- When the client receives this update, it reconciles (corrects) its own prediction based on the server's data. This ensures that the client's view of the game eventually matches the server's, even if there are temporary discrepancies.
- In our example, if the client's prediction was slightly off, the server's update will gently correct the character's position.

State Compression:

- Reducing the amount of data sent over the network can reduce network traffic and improve latency.
- For example, instead of sending the full 3D coordinates of a player's position, you might send a compressed representation or only send updates when the player's position changes significantly.

3. Time Synchronization: Agreeing on the Clock

For many multiplayer games, especially those that rely on precise timing, it's important that all clients have a relatively consistent view of time.

Why it's important:

- Accurate timing of events: For example, ensuring that all players see a bullet hit a target at the same moment.
- Fairness in gameplay: Ensuring that actions happen in the correct order and that players don't have an unfair advantage due to time differences.

Techniques:

- NTP (Network Time Protocol): A standard protocol for synchronizing clocks across the internet. It's often used for general time synchronization, but its accuracy might not be sufficient for very demanding games.
- Custom Time Synchronization Algorithms: Games often implement their own algorithms to refine time synchronization and account for network jitter. These algorithms might involve exchanging timestamps between clients and the server and adjusting local clocks accordingly.

Conceptual Example (Client-Side Prediction)

Let's look at a simplified example to illustrate the basic idea of client-side prediction in Rust:

```rust
Rust


struct Player {
```

```rust
    position: [f32; 2], // 2D position (x, y)

    velocity: [f32; 2], // 2D velocity (speed and
direction)

}




fn predict_position(player: &Player, delta_time:
f32) -> [f32; 2] {

    [

        player.position[0] + player.velocity[0] *
delta_time,

        player.position[1] + player.velocity[1] *
delta_time,

    ]

}




fn main() {

    let mut player = Player {

        position: [0.0, 0.0],

        velocity: [5.0, 0.0], // Moving to the
right at 5.0 units per second
```

```rust
    };



    let delta_time = 0.1; // Simulate a short
time interval (e.g., 0.1 seconds)



    // Simulate client-side prediction

    let predicted_position =
predict_position(&player, delta_time);

    println!("Predicted position: {:?}",
predicted_position);



    // (Later, the server's actual position
arrives and is used to correct the client's
prediction)

}
```

In this example:

- We have a Player struct with position and velocity.
- The predict_position function calculates the player's predicted position based on their current velocity and the time elapsed.
- The main function simulates a simple prediction step.

This code shows how the client can estimate the player's position to provide immediate feedback, even before receiving the authoritative update from the server.

Exercise:

1. Explain the key differences between TCP and UDP and provide specific examples of when each protocol would be most appropriate for use in a multiplayer game scenario.
2. Describe the main challenges of achieving low latency in online multiplayer games, focusing on the factors that contribute to network delay and how they impact the player experience.
3. Write a simple TCP client in Rust that can connect to a server, send a message containing player input, and receive a response, including basic error handling for network connection failures.
4. Explain the concepts of client-side prediction and server reconciliation in detail, describing how they are used to mitigate the effects of network latency and maintain a responsive game experience for players.
5. Research and describe a specific technique for time synchronization in networked games, such as NTP or a custom algorithm, and explain its importance for ensuring fairness and consistency between clients.
6. Design a simplified network protocol for a turn-based strategy game, specifying the types of messages that would need to be exchanged between the client and the server, the information that would be included in each message, and how the protocol would handle game state updates and player actions.

Chapter 11: Tooling and Workflow

Okay, let's talk about making our lives as game developers a bit easier. This chapter is all about tooling and workflow – the processes and tools we use to build, test, and manage our games. Efficient tooling and a smooth workflow can significantly boost productivity and reduce stress.

11.1 Creating Custom Game Development Tools

Okay, let's talk about building tools to make our game development process smoother. This is a big deal because the right tools can save us a lot of time, reduce errors, and really boost our overall productivity.

When we say "custom game development tools," we're talking about programs or scripts that we create specifically to help us with tasks that aren't well-handled by general-purpose software. These tools are tailored to the unique needs of our game and the way we like to work.

Why Create Custom Tools?

- Efficiency: Tools can automate repetitive or tedious tasks, freeing up our time for more creative and challenging work.
- Specialization: Tools can be designed to do exactly what we need, with no unnecessary features or limitations.
- Control: Custom tools give us complete control over the development process, allowing us to adapt them as our needs change.

Examples of Custom Game Development Tools

The range of tools we can create is vast, but here are some of the most common examples:

Level Editors:

- These are tools for designing and creating game levels.
- They can vary in complexity from simple editors that allow you to place objects in a scene to sophisticated tools that handle:
  - Terrain generation
  - Lighting
  - Scripting
  - AI pathfinding

Asset Pipelines:

- These are scripts or programs that automate the process of importing, processing, and organizing game assets (models, textures, sounds, etc.).
- An asset pipeline might:
  - Convert assets from one format to another.
  - Optimize assets for performance.
  - Generate previews of assets.
  - Organize assets into folders.

Animation Editors:

- These tools are used to create and edit character animations.
- They often provide features like:
  - Keyframing (setting poses at specific points in time).
  - Motion capture integration.
  - Animation blending.

Dialogue Editors:

- These tools are designed for writing and managing dialogue trees (the branching conversations that characters have in RPGs or adventure games).
- They can help with:
    - Writing dialogue.
    - Organizing dialogue branches.
    - Testing dialogue flow.

Data Editors:

- Many games rely on large amounts of data (character stats, item properties, enemy behaviors).
- Data editors provide a user-friendly way to create and modify this data, often with features like:
    - Data validation.
    - Search and filtering.
    - Spreadsheet-like interfaces.

Technologies for Creating Tools

You can use a variety of programming languages and frameworks to create custom game development tools. The choice depends on the complexity of the tool, the performance requirements, and your team's expertise.

Rust:

- Rust is an excellent choice for creating powerful and efficient tools, especially for tasks that require high performance or low-level control.
- It's well-suited for tools that process large amounts of data or perform complex calculations.
- GUI libraries like Iced or Egui can be used to create user interfaces for Rust tools.

Python:

- Python is often used for simpler tools or tools that involve a lot of scripting.
- It's relatively easy to learn and has a rich ecosystem of libraries for tasks like:
  - File processing.
  - Data manipulation.
  - Basic GUI development.

Game Engine Tools:

- Many game engines (like Unity or Unreal Engine) provide their own scripting languages and tools for creating editor extensions.
- This can be a convenient option if you're working within a specific engine.

Web Technologies:

- HTML, CSS, and JavaScript can be used to create web-based tools, which can be useful for collaborative workflows.

Example: A Simple Data Editor (Conceptual Rust)

Let's consider a simplified example of how you might create a data editor in Rust. Suppose you're making an RPG, and you need to manage data for various items in the game. Instead of editing this data directly in a raw text file (which could be error-prone), you could create a tool with a graphical interface.

Rust

```rust
use iced::widget::{button, column, row,
text, text_input};

use iced::{Application, Element,
Command, Settings, Theme};

use iced::executor;

use iced::window;

// Define the structure for item data

#[derive(Debug, Clone)]
```

```rust
struct Item {

    name: String,

    description: String,

    attack: i32,

    defense: i32,

}

// Define messages that represent user
actions

#[derive(Debug, Clone)]

enum Message {

    NameChanged(String),

    DescriptionChanged(String),

    AttackChanged(String),
```

```rust
        DefenseChanged(String),

        SaveItem,

        CreateItem,

    }

    struct ItemEditor {

        current_item: Item,

        items: Vec<Item>,

        name_input: String,

        description_input: String,

        attack_input: String,

        defense_input: String,

        error_message: Option<String>,

    }
```

```rust
impl Application for ItemEditor {

    type Executor = executor::Default;

    type Message = Message;

    type Theme = Theme;

    type Flags = ();

    fn new(_flags: ()) -> (Self,
Command<Message>) {

        (

            ItemEditor {

                current_item: Item {

                    name:
String::new(),

                    description: String::new(),

                    attack: 0,
```

```
                    defense: 0,

                },

                items: Vec::new(),

                name_input:
String::new(),

                description_input:
String::new(),

                attack_input:
String::new(),

                defense_input:
String::new(),

                error_message: None,

            },

            Command::none(),

        )
```

```rust
    }

    fn title(&self) -> String {

        String::from("Item Editor")

    }


    fn update(&mut self, message:
Message) -> Command<Message> {

        match message {

            Message::NameChanged(name)
=> {

                self.name_input = name;

                Command::none()

            }


Message::DescriptionChanged(description
) => {
```

```
                self.description_input
= description;


                Command::none()



        }




Message::AttackChanged(attack) => {


                self.attack_input =
attack;


                Command::none()



        }




Message::DefenseChanged(defense) => {


                self.defense_input =
defense;


                Command::none()



        }
```

```rust
Message::SaveItem => {

    // Validation

    if
    self.name_input.is_empty() {

        self.error_message
        = Some("Name cannot be
        empty".to_string());

        return
        Command::none();

    }

    if let Ok(attack) =
    self.attack_input.parse::<i32>() {

        if let Ok(defense)
        = self.defense_input.parse::<i32>() {

            self.current_item = Item {

                name:
                self.name_input.clone(),
```

```
                description:
                self.description_input.clone(),

                                        attack,

                                        defense,

                                };


        self.items.push(self.current_item.clone
());


        self.error_message = None;


                                // Clear input
        fields


        self.name_input.clear();


        self.description_input.clear();
```

```rust
                    self.attack_input.clear();

                    self.defense_input.clear();

                } else {

                    self.error_message = Some("Invalid
                    defense value".to_string());

                }

            } else {

                self.error_message
                    = Some("Invalid attack
                    value".to_string());

            }

            Command::none()
        }

        Message::CreateItem => {
```

```
                // Clear input fields
for creating a new item


self.name_input.clear();


self.description_input.clear();


self.attack_input.clear();


self.defense_input.clear();

                self.error_message =
None;


                Command::none()


        }


    }


}
```

```rust
fn view(&self) -> Element<Message>
{

    let name_input =
text_input("Item Name",
&self.name_input)



.on_input(Message::NameChanged);

    let description_input =
text_input("Description",
&self.description_input)



.on_input(Message::DescriptionChanged);

    let attack_input =
text_input("Attack",
&self.attack_input)



.on_input(Message::AttackChanged);

    let defense_input =
text_input("Defense",
&self.defense_input)
```

```rust
        .on_input(Message::DefenseChanged);

        let save_button = button("Save
Item").on_press(Message::SaveItem);

        let create_button =
button("Create
Item").on_press(Message::CreateItem);

        let mut content = column![

            text("Item
Editor").size(24),

            name_input,

            description_input,

            attack_input,

            defense_input,

            row![save_button,
create_button],

        ];
```

```rust
        if let Some(error) =
&self.error_message {

            content =
content.push(text(error).style(iced::th
eme::Text::Danger));

        }

        content.into()

    }



    fn theme(&self) -> Theme {

        Theme::default()



    }



    fn run(settings:
Settings<Self::Flags>) -> Result<(),
Error>
```

```rust
    where

        Self: Application<Flags =
Self::Flags, Theme Self::Theme,
Executor = Self::Executor>,

        Self::Executor: Executor,

        Self::Theme: StyleSheet,

        Self::Message: 'static,

        Self: 'static,

    {

        // ... (Run the application)

        Ok(())

    }

}

fn main() {
```

```
ItemEditor::run(Settings::default());


    }
```

This Iced example provides a basic framework for a data editor. It allows you to:

- Input item properties (name, description, attack, defense).
- Save items to a list.
- Display error messages for invalid input.
- Create new items.

A more complete data editor would likely involve:

- Displaying a list of existing items.
- Searching and filtering items.
- Loading and saving data to files.
- More robust data validation.

By creating custom tools like this, we can significantly improve our workflow and make the game development process more efficient and enjoyable.

11.2 Automating Build Processes and Testing

Building a game isn't just about writing code. It often involves a sequence of steps: compiling that code, processing assets (like textures and models), packaging everything together, and then testing to make sure it all works. Doing all of this manually every time you make a change gets old *fast*. That's where automation comes in.

Build Automation: Let the Computer Handle It

Build automation tools allow you to define a series of steps that need to be executed to create a working version of your game. Instead of manually running each command, you trigger the whole process with a single command or a click of a button.

What it is:

- It's like giving your computer a recipe for how to build your game. The recipe includes instructions for compiling code, copying files, running scripts, and any other necessary steps.

Common Build Automation Tools:

- Make: A classic and powerful tool, especially common in C and C++ development. It uses "Makefiles" to define build rules and dependencies.
- Cargo: Rust's built-in build system and package manager. It handles compiling, linking, and managing dependencies for Rust projects.
- Bash Scripts: For simpler automation, especially on Unix-like systems (Linux, macOS), you can write scripts in the Bash scripting language. These scripts can execute a sequence of commands.
- Dedicated Build Servers: For large and complex projects, teams often use dedicated build servers (like Jenkins or GitLab CI/CD). These servers can automate builds, run tests, and even deploy the game to different platforms.

Benefits of Build Automation:

- Time Savings: Automating the build process saves developers a lot of time, especially when making frequent changes.
- Consistency: It ensures that the build process is consistent, reducing the risk of errors caused by manual steps.
- Reduced Errors: Automation minimizes human error in the build process.
- Parallelization: Some build tools can parallelize build tasks, speeding up the process.

Continuous Integration (CI): Automatic Checks

Continuous Integration (CI) takes build automation a step further. It's a practice where code changes are automatically built and tested whenever they're pushed to a version control system (like Git).

What it is:

- Every time a developer commits code, the CI system:
    - Checks out the latest code.
    - Builds the game.
    - Runs automated tests.
    - Reports the results.

CI Tools:

- Popular CI tools include:
    - Jenkins: A very flexible and widely used open-source CI server.

- GitLab CI/CD: CI/CD (Continuous Integration/Continuous Delivery) tools built into GitLab.
- GitHub Actions: CI/CD platform integrated with GitHub.

Benefits of CI:

- Early Error Detection: CI helps to catch errors early in the development process, before they become more difficult and expensive to fix.
- Improved Code Quality: By running automated tests, CI ensures that new code changes don't break existing functionality.
- Faster Development Cycles: CI reduces the time it takes to build and test the game, allowing developers to iterate more quickly.
- Increased Collaboration: CI provides a central place to view the build and test status, improving communication within the team.

Automated Testing: Ensuring Correctness

Automated testing is the practice of writing code that tests your game code. Instead of manually playing through the game to check for bugs, you write tests that automatically verify that different parts of your code are working as expected.

What it is:

- Automated tests are code that executes other code and checks if the output or behavior is correct.
- There are different types of tests, such as:

- **Unit Tests:** Tests individual functions or modules in isolation.
- **Integration Tests:** Tests how different parts of the code work together.
- **System Tests:** Tests the entire system from end to end.

Rust's Testing Support:

- Rust has built-in support for unit tests. You can write tests directly within your Rust code using the #[test] attribute.
- Crates like assert_approx_eq (for floating-point comparisons) and rstest (for parameterized tests) can extend Rust's testing capabilities.

Benefits of Automated Testing:

- Increased Confidence: Automated tests give you confidence that your code is working correctly.
- Reduced Bugs: Tests help to catch bugs early in the development process.
- Easier Refactoring: You can refactor your code (change its structure) without worrying about breaking existing functionality, because the tests will catch any regressions.
- Improved Maintainability: Tests make it easier to maintain your code over time, as you can easily verify that changes haven't introduced new problems.

Example: Automating a Rust Game Build with Cargo

Cargo, Rust's build system, provides a lot of automation out of the box.

Rust

```
// Cargo.toml (Project configuration)


[package]


name = "my_game"


version = "0.1.0"


edition = "2021"


# See more keys and their definitions
at
https://doc.rust-lang.org/cargo/referen
ce/manifest.html


[dependencies]


# Add your game's dependencies here


[dev-dependencies]
```

```
# Add dependencies used only for
development (e.g., testing)
```

Build Commands:

- cargo build: Compiles your game.
- cargo run: Compiles and runs your game.
- cargo test: Runs all the tests in your project.
- cargo check: Quickly checks for compile errors without building.

Example: A Simple Rust Unit Test

Rust

```rust
// src/lib.rs


pub fn add(a: i32, b: i32) -> i32 {


    a + b


}


#[cfg(test)] // Only compile this code
when running tests


mod tests {


    use super::*; // Bring the code
from the outer module into scope
```

```rust
    #[test] // This attribute marks a
function as a test

    fn it_adds_two() {

        assert_eq!(add(2, 2), 4);

    }

    #[test]

    fn it_adds_negative_numbers() {

        assert_eq!(add(-1, 5), 4);

    }

}
```

In a real game project, you'd have many more tests, covering
different aspects of your game logic.

Example: Continuous Integration with GitHub Actions (Conceptual)

You can configure GitHub Actions to automatically build and test your Rust game whenever you push code to your GitHub repository.

YAML

```yaml
# .github/workflows/ci.yml (Workflow
definition)

name: CI

on:

  push:

    branches: [ "main" ]

  pull_request:

    branches: [ "main" ]

  jobs:

    build_and_test:
```

```yaml
    runs-on: ubuntu-latest # Run on a
Linux virtual machine

    steps:

        - uses: actions/checkout@v3 #
Checkout the code

        - uses: actions/cache@v3

        with:

            path: ~/.cargo/registry

            key: ${{ runner.os
}}-cargo-registry-${{
hashFiles('Cargo.lock') }}

        - uses: actions/cache@v3

        with:

            path: ~/.cargo/git

            key: ${{ runner.os
}}-cargo-git-${{
hashFiles('Cargo.lock') }}
```

```
- name: Install Rust

  uses:
dtolnay/rust-toolchain@stable

- name: Build

  run: cargo build --release

- name: Run tests

  run: cargo test
```

This is a simplified example, but it shows how GitHub Actions can automate the build and test process.

By embracing automation, we can free ourselves from repetitive tasks, improve the quality of our code, and accelerate the development of our games.

11.3 Streamlining the Development Workflow

A well-defined and streamlined workflow can significantly impact a game development team's productivity, communication, and overall success. It's about creating a system that helps everyone work together effectively and reduces friction in the development process.

Here are some key elements of a good development workflow:

1. Version Control: The Time Machine for Code

Version control systems (VCS) are absolutely essential for any software development project, and game development is no exception. Git is the most popular VCS, so we'll focus on that.

What it is:

- Git allows you to track every change made to your code and other files (like assets) over time.
- It's like having a time machine for your project, allowing you to go back to previous versions if needed.

Key Concepts:

- Repository (Repo): The central location where all the files and their history are stored.
- Commit: A snapshot of your changes at a specific point in time. Each commit has a message describing what you changed.
- Branch: A separate line of development. You can create branches to work on new features or bug fixes without affecting the main codebase.
- Merge: Combining changes from one branch into another.
- Pull Request: A request to merge changes, often used to facilitate code reviews.

Why it's crucial:

- Collaboration: Git makes it easy for multiple developers to work on the same project without conflicts.
- History Tracking: You can see exactly who changed what and when, which is invaluable for debugging.
- Experimentation: Branches allow you to experiment with new features without risking the stability of the main codebase.
- Reversion: If you introduce a bug, you can easily revert to a previous working version.

Real-world example:

- When you're working on a document with someone using Google Docs, it automatically saves changes and keeps track of who made what edits. Git does this but in a much more powerful and controlled way for code.

2. Code Style and Formatting: Consistency is Key

Consistent coding style is incredibly important, especially when working in a team. It makes the code easier to read, understand, and maintain.

What it is:

- Code style refers to the conventions you follow when writing code, such as:
    - Indentation (how many spaces or tabs to use).
    - Naming conventions (how to name variables, functions, etc.).
    - Spacing and line breaks.

o Comments.

Benefits:

- Readability: Consistent style makes the code easier to read and follow.
- Maintainability: It's easier to understand and modify code written by someone else.
- Reduced Errors: Consistent style can help to prevent certain types of errors.

Code Formatting Tools:

- To enforce code style, you can use code formatting tools that automatically format your code according to predefined rules.
- Rust has a built-in tool called rustfmt that can format Rust code.

Real-world example:

- Think about how a well-formatted document is easier to read than one with inconsistent spacing and fonts. Code formatting does the same thing for your code.

3. Code Reviews: Fresh Eyes, Better Code

Code reviews are a practice where developers review each other's code before it's integrated into the main codebase.

What it is:

- A developer who wrote some code submits it for review by other team members.
- Reviewers read the code, look for potential errors, suggest improvements, and provide feedback.

Benefits:

- Bug Detection: Reviews can catch bugs that the original developer might have missed.
- Knowledge Sharing: They help to spread knowledge of the codebase and coding practices within the team.
- Improved Code Quality: Reviews encourage developers to write cleaner, more maintainable code.
- Team Cohesion: They foster collaboration and communication within the team.

Real-world example:

- In scientific research, papers are often peer-reviewed by other scientists before they are published. Code reviews serve a similar purpose in software development.

4. Communication Tools: Staying Connected

Effective communication is crucial for any team project, and game development is no exception.

What it is:

- Using tools and platforms to facilitate communication between team members.

Examples:

- Chat Applications (Slack, Discord): For quick questions, discussions, and sharing updates.
- Email: For more formal communication or sharing documents.
- Video Conferencing (Zoom, Google Meet): For meetings and discussions.

Why it's important:

- Keeps everyone informed about project status and progress.
- Facilitates quick resolution of issues and roadblocks.
- Improves collaboration and teamwork.

Real-world example:

- Think about how teams in offices use tools like Slack or Microsoft Teams to communicate throughout the day.

5. Project Management: Keeping Things Organized

Game development projects can be complex, involving many tasks, deadlines, and dependencies. Project management tools help to keep everything organized and on track.

What it is:

- Using software or systems to:
    - Break down the project into smaller tasks.
    - Assign tasks to team members.
    - Track progress.
    - Manage deadlines.
    - Identify and address potential problems.

Examples:

- Trello: A visual and flexible tool that uses cards and boards.
- Jira: A powerful and feature-rich tool often used for bug tracking and agile project management.
- Asana: A task management tool that emphasizes collaboration and workflow.

Why it's important:

- Improves organization and planning.
- Helps to meet deadlines.
- Increases team accountability.
- Reduces the risk of projects going over budget or behind schedule.

Real-world example:

- Construction companies use project management software to track the progress of building a house, from laying the foundation to finishing the interior.

Example: A Streamlined Rust Development Workflow

Here's a simplified example of how these workflow elements might come together in a Rust game development project:

Version Control (Git):

- Developers use Git to manage the game's code and assets.
- They create branches for new features and bug fixes.
- They use pull requests to review each other's code before merging it into the main branch.

Code Style and Formatting (rustfmt):

- The team uses rustfmt to automatically format their Rust code, ensuring consistency.

Automated Testing (Cargo):

- Developers write unit tests and integration tests to verify the correctness of their code.
- They use cargo test to run these tests.

Continuous Integration (GitHub Actions):

- GitHub Actions is configured to automatically:
    - Build the game whenever code is pushed to the repository.
    - Run all the tests.
    - Report the build and test results.

Communication (Discord):

- The team uses Discord to communicate throughout the day, share updates, and discuss issues.

Project Management (Jira):

- Jira is used to track tasks, assign them to team members, and manage deadlines.

By implementing these workflow practices, game development teams can create a more efficient, collaborative, and enjoyable development process, which ultimately leads to better games.

Chapter 12: Packaging and Distribution

Okay, let's talk about the final steps in the game development process: getting your game into the hands of players. This chapter covers packaging your game, distributing it through various channels, and optimizing it for different platforms.

12.1 Cross-Platform Builds

Okay, let's talk about making our games playable on more than just one type of computer or device. This is what we mean by "cross-platform development," and it's a big topic in the game industry.

In today's market, many developers want their games to reach as many players as possible. This often means releasing the game on several different platforms.

Common platforms include:

Desktop Computers:

- Windows (the most common platform for PC gaming)
- macOS (Apple computers)
- Linux (an open-source operating system)

Consoles:

- PlayStation (Sony)
- Xbox (Microsoft)
- Nintendo Switch

Mobile Devices:

- Android (Google)
- iOS (Apple)

Web Browsers:

- Games can sometimes be played directly in a web browser using technologies like WebAssembly.

Cross-platform development is the process of writing your game code in a way that allows it to be compiled and run on these different platforms. Instead of writing separate versions of your game for each platform, you aim to create a single codebase that can be adapted.

The Challenges of Going Cross-Platform

Cross-platform development comes with its own set of challenges, though:

Platform Differences:

- Each platform has its own operating system, hardware, and software.
- These differences can affect everything from how you handle input to how you render graphics.
- For example, Windows uses DirectX for graphics, while macOS uses Metal, and Linux often uses Vulkan.

Graphics APIs:

- As mentioned, different platforms might use different graphics APIs, which are the software libraries that allow you to communicate with the GPU (graphics processing unit).
- This means you might need to use an abstraction layer (a layer of code that sits between your game and the underlying API) to handle these differences.

Input Handling:

- You need to support various input devices:
  - Keyboards and mice (on desktop computers)
  - Gamepads (on consoles)
  - Touchscreens (on mobile devices)
- You might need to adapt your controls or UI for each device.

File System Differences:

- The way files are organized and accessed can vary between operating systems.
- File paths, directory structures, and file permissions can all be different.

Build Systems and Packaging:

- Each platform might require a different build system (the software that compiles your code) and packaging format (the way your game is distributed).

Rust's Role in Cross-Platform Development

Rust is actually quite well-suited for cross-platform development, thanks to some of its core features and the ecosystem of crates (Rust libraries).

Abstraction:

- Rust provides abstractions that help you write code that's not tied to a specific platform.
- For example, Rust's standard library provides platform-independent ways to work with files and threads.

Crates:

- Crates like winit and sdl2 offer cross-platform windowing and input handling, allowing you to create windows and respond to user input in a way that works on multiple operating systems.
- Libraries like wgpu provide a cross-platform graphics API, enabling you to write rendering code once and run it on different GPUs.

Cargo:

- Rust's build system, Cargo, can handle compiling your code for different target platforms. This process is called cross-compilation.

Example: Cross-Compiling with Cargo

Cargo makes cross-compiling relatively straightforward. You'll need to install the necessary toolchains (collections of compiler and linker tools) for each target platform.

Here's a simplified example of how you might cross-compile a Rust game:

Bash

```
# Add targets (these are just examples,
you'll need to research the correct
targets for your needs)




# For 64-bit Windows


rustup target add x86_64-pc-windows-gnu


# For 64-bit macOS


rustup target add x86_64-apple-darwin


# For 64-bit Linux
```

```
rustup target add
x86_64-unknown-linux-gnu


# Build for Windows (the --release flag
optimizes the build)


cargo build --target
x86_64-pc-windows-gnu --release


# Build for macOS


cargo build --target
x86_64-apple-darwin --release


# Build for Linux


cargo build --target
x86_64-unknown-linux-gnu --release
```

This example shows how to use Cargo to build your Rust code for Windows, macOS, and Linux. You would then need to handle platform-specific details like packaging and distribution separately.

Important Considerations for Cross-Platform Development

- Testing: Thoroughly test your game on each target platform to ensure it works correctly.
- Performance: Optimize your game for each platform's hardware.
- Input Mapping: Provide appropriate input methods and control schemes for different devices.
- UI Adaptation: Design your UI to scale and adapt to different screen resolutions and aspect ratios.
- Platform-Specific Features: You might want to take advantage of unique features on certain platforms (e.g., haptic feedback on a controller).

Cross-platform development is a complex but rewarding endeavor. Rust's features and the growing ecosystem of Rust crates make it a viable option for creating games that can reach a wide audience.

12.2 Game Distribution Strategies

Once you've finished developing your game, you need to decide how you're going to make it available to the world. There are several different approaches, each with its own advantages and disadvantages.

Here's a breakdown of the common game distribution strategies:

1. Digital Distribution Platforms: The Online Marketplaces

Digital distribution platforms are online stores where players can purchase and download games directly to their computers or devices.[1] These platforms have become the dominant way to distribute games, especially for PC and mobile.[2]

Examples:

PC:

- Steam: The largest digital distribution platform for PC games.[3] It has a massive user base and provides tools for game updates, community features, and more.[4]
- Epic Games Store: A platform that has grown in popularity by offering exclusive titles and giving developers a larger share of revenue.
- GOG (Good Old Games): A platform that focuses on selling DRM-free (Digital Rights Management-free) games.[5]

Consoles:

- PlayStation Store (PlayStation)[6]
- Xbox Store (Xbox)[7]
- Nintendo eShop (Nintendo Switch)[8]

Mobile:

- App Store (iOS)[9]
- Google Play Store (Android)[10]

What they offer:

- Payment Processing: The platforms handle the financial transactions, so you don't need to set up your own payment system.
- Digital Rights Management (DRM): Some platforms offer DRM to protect your game from piracy (though DRM is a controversial topic).[11]
- Downloads and Updates: They provide the infrastructure for players to download your game and receive updates.[12]
- Community Features: Many platforms include features like forums, reviews, and social networking tools, which can help you connect with players.
- Marketing and Discovery: Being on a popular platform can increase the visibility of your game and help players discover it.

Considerations:

- Revenue Share: Platforms typically take a percentage of your game's sales as a fee. This percentage varies between platforms.
- Platform Requirements: Each platform has its own technical and content requirements that your game must meet.[13]
- Curation: Some platforms curate the games they sell, meaning your game might need to be approved before it's listed.

2. Direct Sales: Going It Alone

Direct sales involve selling your game directly to players, without relying on a third-party platform.[14] This usually means selling it from your own website or online store.

What it involves:

- Payment Processing: You'll need to set up your own system to handle payments (e.g., using a payment gateway like Stripe or PayPal).
- Digital Distribution: You'll need to provide a way for players to download the game files (e.g., through your website or a file hosting service).[15]
- Customer Support: You'll be responsible for providing customer support to players who have issues with your game.

Advantages:

- Higher Revenue Share: You keep a larger percentage of the sales revenue.
- More Control: You have more control over the pricing, marketing, and distribution of your game.
- Direct Relationship with Players: You can build a closer relationship with your players and get direct feedback.

Disadvantages:

- Lower Visibility: It can be harder for players to discover your game if it's not on a popular platform.
- Increased Responsibility: You're responsible for handling all aspects of sales and distribution.

- Technical Challenges: Setting up payment processing and secure downloads can be technically challenging.

3. Physical Distribution: Boxes and Discs

Physical distribution involves selling your game on physical media, such as:

- Discs (CDs, DVDs, Blu-rays)[16]
- Cartridges (for consoles like the Nintendo Switch)

This was the dominant way to distribute games in the past, but it's less common today, especially for indie developers.

What it involves:

- Manufacturing: Producing the physical copies of your game.
- Distribution to Retailers: Getting your game into stores.
- Logistics: Managing inventory, shipping, and returns.

Challenges:

- High Costs: Manufacturing and distribution can be very expensive.[17]
- Logistics Complexity: Managing physical inventory and shipping can be complex.
- Retailer Dependence: You're reliant on retailers to sell your game.

When it might be used:

- For very large-budget games.

- For games with a strong physical collector's market.
- Sometimes in niche markets.

4. Early Access: A Work in Progress

Early Access involves releasing your game in an unfinished state to players.[18] Players can purchase and play the game while it's still in development.

What it offers:

- Feedback: You can get valuable feedback from players to help shape the development of your game.
- Community Building: You can build a community of players around your game early on.
- Funding: Early Access can provide a source of revenue to support development.[19]

Considerations:

- Player Expectations: You need to be transparent about the state of your game and manage player expectations.
- Development Commitment: You need to be committed to continuing development and delivering on your promises.
- Platform Restrictions: Not all platforms have robust Early Access programs. Steam is the most well-known.

5. Free-to-Play: Playing for Free, Paying for More

Free-to-play (F2P) involves releasing your game for free and generating revenue through other means.[20]

Monetization Methods:

- In-App Purchases: Selling virtual items or content within the game.
- Advertising: Displaying ads to players.
- Subscriptions: Charging players a recurring fee for access to content or features.[21]

Considerations:

- Game Design: Your game needs to be designed to support the chosen monetization model.
- Ethical Considerations: It's important to avoid predatory or manipulative monetization practices.

Choosing the Right Strategy

The best distribution strategy for your game depends on factors such as:

- Budget: How much money do you have to spend on marketing and distribution?
- Target Audience: Where does your target audience typically buy games?
- Game Genre: Some genres are better suited to certain distribution models (e.g., mobile games are often F2P).
- Development Stage: Is your game finished, or are you looking for early feedback?

By carefully considering these factors, you can choose a distribution strategy that maximizes your game's reach and success.

12.3 Optimizing for Different Platforms

When you create a game, you want it to be enjoyed by as many people as possible. However, the hardware and software capabilities vary greatly across different platforms. A game that runs smoothly on a powerful gaming PC might struggle on a mobile phone or a less powerful console. Therefore, optimization is key.

Here's a breakdown of the main optimization considerations:

1. Performance Optimization: Making It Run Smoothly

Performance optimization is about ensuring that your game runs at an acceptable frame rate on each target platform. Frame rate is the number of images the game displays per second, and a higher frame rate generally means smoother gameplay.

The Challenge:

- Different platforms have different processing power, memory, and graphics capabilities.
- A complex scene that's easy for a high-end PC to render might overwhelm a mobile phone's GPU.

Optimization Techniques:

- Graphics Settings: Provide adjustable graphics settings that allow players to customize the game's visuals to match their hardware. This is common on PC games, where players can choose between "low," "medium," "high," and "ultra" settings.
- Resolution Scaling: Allow players to adjust the game's rendering resolution. Lowering the resolution reduces the

number of pixels that need to be drawn, improving performance.

- Level of Detail (LOD): Render objects with lower detail when they are far away from the camera. This reduces the number of polygons that need to be processed.
- Culling: Avoid rendering objects that are not currently visible (e.g., objects behind walls or outside the camera's view).
- Shader Optimization: Write efficient shaders (programs that run on the GPU) to minimize their computational cost.
- Memory Management: Optimize memory usage to prevent slowdowns caused by excessive memory allocation or swapping.
- CPU Optimization: Identify and optimize CPU-intensive tasks, such as physics simulations or AI calculations.

Profiling Tools:

- Profiling tools are essential for identifying performance bottlenecks.
- These tools allow you to measure how long different parts of your code take to execute and pinpoint areas that need optimization.
- Game engines and development platforms often provide their own profiling tools.

Real-world example:

- Many PC games allow players to adjust settings like texture quality, shadow resolution, and anti-aliasing to achieve a good balance between visual quality and performance.

2. Input Handling: Controlling the Game

Different platforms use different input devices, and your game needs to handle them appropriately.

The Challenge:

- Desktop computers use keyboards and mice.
- Consoles use gamepads.
- Mobile devices use touchscreens.
- Each device has different strengths and weaknesses, and players have different preferences.

Optimization Techniques:

- Input Abstraction: Create an abstraction layer that maps input from different devices to consistent game actions (e.g., "jump," "attack," "move"). This makes it easier to write code that handles input from various sources.
- Customizable Controls: Allow players to remap controls to their liking. This is especially important for accessibility.
- Touch Controls: For mobile games, design intuitive and responsive touch controls. Consider using virtual buttons, gestures, and context-sensitive controls.
- Gamepad Support: Ensure that your UI and gameplay are fully navigable with a gamepad, as some players might prefer it even on PC.

Real-world example:

- Many PC games automatically detect the presence of a gamepad and switch to a gamepad-friendly control scheme.

3. Screen Resolution and Aspect Ratio: Adapting the View

Platforms have varying screen resolutions and aspect ratios (the ratio of width to height). Your game needs to adapt to these differences to ensure it looks good on all screens.

The Challenge:

- A UI designed for a widescreen monitor might look stretched or cramped on a mobile phone.
- Text and UI elements need to scale appropriately to remain readable.

Optimization Techniques:

- UI Scaling: Design your UI to scale automatically based on the screen resolution. Use relative sizes and positions instead of fixed pixel values.
- Aspect Ratio Correction: Adjust the game's field of view or UI layout to accommodate different aspect ratios.
- Resolution Independence: Render your UI and game elements at a higher resolution and then scale them down to the target resolution. This can improve visual quality.

Real-world example:

- Modern web browsers automatically scale web pages to fit different screen sizes and orientations. Game UIs often use similar techniques.

4. File Formats and Packaging: Platform-Specific Needs

Each platform may have specific requirements for file formats and how your game is packaged and distributed.

The Challenge:

- Windows uses .exe files.
- macOS uses .app bundles.
- Android uses .apk files.
- Consoles have their own proprietary packaging formats.

Optimization Techniques:

- Asset Compression: Compress game assets (textures, models, audio) to reduce file size and loading times.
- Platform-Specific File Formats: Use file formats that are optimized for each platform's hardware (e.g., specific texture compression formats).
- Packaging Tools: Use the appropriate tools to package your game for each platform's distribution method (e.g., creating installers for Windows, building APKs for Android).

Real-world example:

- Mobile games are often packaged as .apk files for Android and .ipa files for iOS, which are specifically designed for those operating systems.

Example: Optimizing for Mobile (Conceptual)

Mobile devices present unique challenges due to their limited processing power, memory, and battery life. Here are some common optimization techniques for mobile games:

- Lower-Resolution Textures: Use smaller or lower-resolution textures to reduce memory usage and improve rendering performance.
- Simplified Models: Use models with fewer polygons to reduce the workload on the GPU.
- Reduced Draw Calls: Minimize the number of draw calls (commands sent to the GPU) to reduce overhead. This can be achieved by batching rendering operations.
- Power-Efficient Rendering: Use rendering techniques that consume less power, such as using simpler shaders and avoiding complex lighting effects.
- Touch Controls: Design intuitive and responsive touch controls that are optimized for mobile devices.

By carefully considering these optimization factors, you can ensure that your game runs smoothly and looks good on a wide range of platforms, providing a great experience for all players.

Conclusion

We've covered a lot of ground in this book, from the foundational principles of Rust to the advanced techniques that empower you to build compelling games. We've explored Rust's memory management, delved into architectural patterns, and tackled the complexities of rendering, input, and physics. We've also discussed the importance of tooling, workflow, and distribution in bringing your game to fruition.

The journey of game development is a multifaceted one, demanding both technical prowess and creative vision. Rust, with its blend of performance and safety, offers a robust platform for this endeavor. It allows you to write efficient code that can handle the demanding computations of game logic, while also providing the safeguards to prevent common errors that can plague game development.

However, this book is just the beginning. Game development is a constantly evolving field. New technologies, techniques, and trends emerge regularly. The key to continued success lies in your willingness to learn, experiment, and adapt.

I encourage you to take the knowledge and skills you've gained here and apply them to your own projects. Build small games, experiment with different techniques, and don't be afraid to make mistakes. That's how you truly learn and grow as a game developer.

Remember that game development is also a collaborative art. Connect with other developers, share your experiences, and learn from each other. The game development community is a vibrant and supportive one, and you'll find a wealth of knowledge and inspiration within it.

Finally, and perhaps most importantly, have fun! Game development is a challenging but incredibly rewarding pursuit. It allows you to bring your creative visions to life and share them with the world. Embrace the challenges, celebrate the successes, and never stop creating.

I wish you the best in your game development adventures!